A KINGDOM
of
CONTROVERSY

A KINGDOM
of
CONTROVERSY

By

La'Rahz – Roslyn O'Flaherty Isaacs

iUniverse

A KINGDOM OF CONTROVERSY

iUniverse books may be ordered through booksellers or by contacting:

iUniverse
1663 Liberty Drive
Bloomington, IN 47403
www.iuniverse.com
844-349-9409

Because of the dynamic nature of the Internet, any web addresses or links contained in this book may have changed since publication and may no longer be valid. The views expressed in this work are solely those of the author and do not necessarily reflect the views of the publisher, and the publisher hereby disclaims any responsibility for them.

Any people depicted in stock imagery provided by Thinkstock are models, and such images are being used for illustrative purposes only.
Certain stock imagery © Thinkstock.

ISBN: 978-1-4759-0531-1 (sc)
ISBN: 978-1-4759-0532-8 (e)

Print information available on the last page.

iUniverse rev. date: 03/27/2012

Being held hostage
in that
plantation mentality
is a great enslavement
that is not our earthly mission . . .

La'Rahz
Story telling poet.

DEDICATION

THIS BOOK IS DEDICATED TO
MAGIC FEET
*My best friend in the world,
I love you.*

*La'Rahz ~ R.E.O.I.
Storytelling Poet*

*We praise you for touching our lives.
You know who God is.
We want you to know
your spirit is with the Lord now.
He lays you to rest with a peaceful soul.
The angels made you our guardian so you can bring our faith level up,
as you
dwell in the house of the Lord!
You left us quite too soon, Magic Feet.*

TABLE OF CONTENTS

THANK YOU SO MUCH

I would like to give special thanks. To Mama Glo. for her kindness and assistance in helping with the formatting processes for this book.

Love you Glo.
LaRahz R.E.O.I

INTRODUCTION

La'Rahz' poetry shows her ingenious narration through conceived mental images. She hopes to take you from the unspoken word to the word while using freedom of speech and revealing life through fiction communication. She will make you feel the catch, the hook and the twists as stories unfold. You will feel detailed knowledge of struggle, scrutiny and passion. With an element of surprise. This book is a fiction artistic expression. That will not determine what the world says should be said, for the worlds empowerment. Imagine the spirit of life ousted and being controlled as you look for new beginnings of courage without betrayal. A Kingdom of Controversy leaves you room for your own opinions and beliefs. The fiction described details, names, characters and places are products of author's imagination. Perceive with caution! This book will make you feel inferior without consent. Its significance is left to your discretion. Never lose focus on the spirit of freedom, love and joy. Don't relate fiction events to any person living or officially pronounced dead. It is entirely coincidental. Time to step out of the box! Look for the message in her controversial, climatic collection of poetry and short stories from a different dimension. Use your mind rationally to contradict her thoughts, ideas and any notions you may have . . . Make your own purchasing decision! Mature Adult Contents! Some parts of this book contains adult, contents that is not suitable for children. Parental guidance is advised due to mature subjects, that maybe inappropriate . . . LaRahz's book is not like no other book on the market. A Kingdom of Controversy is truly one to be read. You will read a full conscious choice of life where common concerns arise. Taking your mind to a realm of living, to decide if this books contents, is genocide with or without justice? You will read a continued discharge of territorial offenses. That is based on details and actions of the dramatic plots. La'Rahz lets her poetry grab your feeling and emotions. It's time to observe the world through imaginative writing. Take a trip to an informal pathway of story telling poetry. That is not restricted to poetry norm. It will take you to a place that doesn't dictate what the world says, you're supposed to walk, talk and act like. The controversy has a structured form that is not meant for retaliation. It is to ensure readers that we can avoid confinement of the standard pattern of life. The conflict and thoughts can be good or bad. You will have a choice to keep your mind rational. It will keep you with a comprehensibility of its heart felt experiences. The Kingdom Of Controversy by La'Rahz ~ R.E.O.I. is a walk you will identify with alone. Be ataman about this Kingdom Of Thought. You will be able to give clarity on where your true beliefs come from. Use your own free will. Remember this book is not meant to keep people blind to the ethics and reality of the way some people live. Open your mind and remove yourself from cultural mishap. This world cannot become a mental institution. You can go into the Kingdom Of Controversy, but can you come out with the word in this kingdom of thought? La'Rahz writes to liberate people . . .

La'Rahz - Roslyn O'Flaherty Isaacs

HOW WE SURVIVED

Poverty-stricken!
You invited me to lunch.
Spiced ham sliced so thin
You could see through it.
Kool-Aid in a jelly jar.
I remember this lunch,
my Mama use to make that.
Now she reminds me to turn the light
off in the kitchen or the roaches will come
out. Exterminator came yesterday to give
them a bath. The poison did not work.
Had me take everything out of the cabinets,
for what? Now I must run down to the
bodega to get the Black Flag.
The situation has gotten worse.
I wasn't born with a silver spoon in my
mouth. My birth place is America.
I feel I'm a first class citizen.
I'm not a stranger to poverty and struggle.
This is how we survived. I'm stranded in life's
games. I sleep with the pee-the-bed boy. Piss
all over me. That's it!
New strategy needed for sleeping arrangements.
It seems pointless to even let the asshole in the same
bed. He needs to sleep on the toilet.
Maybe that will put some emphasis on the situation.
The ironing cord just isn't working. I can't
keep going to school smelling like piss.
My dad's an Uncle Tom at work
so that he can get a paycheck to feed his family.
Uncle Tomming, for half the normal wages on a
full-time job that only perpetuates enslavement.
His culture is disconnected from his soul,
yet he looks for leadership
and a connection to justice

in this land of opportunity.
My Godfather visits us.
He acts like he's our daddy.
He's a womanizer. My father's best friend.
Walking around like he's ghetto fabulous.
Done brought the family some welfare cheese
and pork in the can. "NASTY," if I regurgitate
on the pork. I'm going to get the taste slapped out
my mouth. I'd rather eat a ketchup or mayonnaise
sandwich. Castor Oil and Cod Liver Oil were
'nasty too', but we never had a cold.
Ironing cord, strap, or a switch off the tree.
I wonder today which one it will be.
This isn't even considered child abuse.
I stay getting my ass whipped,
because of tattling neighbors.
Pay parties in the basement.
Gambling to pay rent.
Blue lights, grinding on the wall.
Old Mister, can in the hand sucking
down his beer. One beer over a six pack
and he's straight for the night.
Let's not forget Swiss Up,
Thunder Bird and Boones Farm Wine.
Cotton Club, Boston Road Ballroom,
and Savoy Manor
is where my Dad use to sneak off to
and get his party on.
Mr. Boroughs is our neighborhood cop.
He is a married man.
He walks the beat on my block.
He will make you pay a fine
just for walking on the grass
or hanging in the hall corridor in the building.
His lover is an addict.
Her name is Ms. Margaret.
Ms. Margaret is a prostitute and a lesbian.
Supports her family

as a GO-GO Dancer and a number runner.
She dances on stage butt naked
wearing GO-GO Boots.
Ms. Margaret dances in our local bar.
She collects the almighty dollar!
I wonder if Mr. Boroughs is her pimp?
War junkies our heroes,
with dope fiend mentalities.
Looking for their pusher.
Pothead lit up from a joint.
Liquor mouths killing each other over
chicken bones. Bell-bottoms, Afro puffs
and peace power picks.
"Right on" to the brothers and the sisters.
R&B, Rock n Roll with a little soul.
Mama swears by hand-me-downs.
She thinks spray starch
and hand-me-downs make you look on point.
All you have to do
is wipe down your patent leather shoes
with a little Vaseline.
Mama always brought us Skips and Decks sneakers.
Anything on sale at Tom McCann's shoe store.
I wanted Pro Keds or Chuck Taylors.
My brother loves his PF Flyers.
They look better than his Buster Browns.
I could not stand the, thrift shops.
When Mama finished shopping, we
would go to Carvels for ice cream.
Mama's sitting in the corner
sewing up the holes in her drawers,
Pinning the elastic back on.
Knowing damn well,
it's time for them to go in the garbage
along with her shoes.
The hole in the soles of her shoes
has card board over it.
So her feet don't touch the ground.

Shooting craps, red light green light, one-two-three!
Kick the Can, Hop Scotch and Johnny on the Pony.
I even know how to do the funky chicken!
Don't forget run, catch and kiss.
I'm going home to take my brother outside.
After he watches Captain Kangaroo and Mr. Magoo.
His favorite television character is Lamb Chop.
Time to sit on the bench
and listen to 107.5 R&B Classis Soul.
Gangs' blacks against the blacks.
We fight amongst ourselves.
My Grammy walks around with lye in a
Soda pop bottle. She keeps it in the bottom
of her pocket book. She'll eat your ass up
alive. She doesn't play.
Domestic violence, I don't get it.
Is this all part of surviving or existing?
A death zone with killing.
Folks say we live in the ghetto.
Mama says ghetto is a state of mind.
So what are we living in?
Mama's friends are by talking,
trying to understand why people feel
it's necessary to use racism against one another.
In a negative matter toward others.
(I wonder if this has anything to do with derogation?)
I asked what is racism.
Mama said,
"What I told you about being in grown
folks business?" "Respect your elders,
children should be seen and not heard."
"Go sit down somewhere."
"Get a book and don't be disrespectful."
"Remember, I'm not your friend".
My mom's real old school.
My mother is active in the civil rights movement.
Her church family is always protesting
and marching for different causes.

They have been on TV, the local news station.
Fighting for school buses to bus children in poor
communities. To rich neighborhoods to get a better
education. Yes, education is forever!
They marched one time for financial freedom.
I guess I better grow up quick so I can get mine.
Not that I have to keep up with the Joneses.
History can't repeat itself.
My Massa won't be welfare.
I'm not ignorant.
This won't be genocide.
Reality has set in. I will survive!
My neighborhood has organized
crime hustlers, pimps and number runners.
Jail time offering drug programs
and mental institutions opposed to incarceration.
Our brothers in jail for health benefits,
three meals, a cot and an education.
Some people become religious.
The streets still have loan sharks.
Human interaction of prostitution,
narcotics and gambling.
Gays beaten, and terrorized
because of people's stupidity.
Gays in the closet, fighting in the military.
Race and genders are misunderstood.
Men on my corner are inebriated.
I can't tolerate listening and living dumb shit . . .
THIS IS HOW WE SURVIVED.
This was the norm,
when people grew up in my generation.
Living in what some call
"a place of dysfunction."
The norm is not destructions,
but the reality to overcome my struggle.
I may be bruised as the psycho paths of the world
give regulations. Bruised but not fragmented.
This life was hard, I am commonsensical.

My hard times have made me a better human being.
I made it through my reality,
which gave me wisdom and strengths.
I was able to understand the infinite
possibility to use my faith.
Yet, I felt no political stability!
I was liberated in my survival skills.
The revelation of hard times is here.
I will not live beyond my means.

I must be content within myself!
This can't be my destiny.
I'm just waiting for the day.
That I will be free!
I still have my integrity!
I don't have to change, just adjust.
I am only human . . .
Regardless of how we survived!

La'Rahz - Roslyn O'Flaherty Isaacs

MY RIGHTS

Give me my rights back!
The right to speak freely.
You see, I've been threatened to be held in contempt
For not keeping my mouth shut.
Disrespecting a court legislator.
A qualified authorized judge says,
one more word, and he'll be forced to hold me
in contempt. I wasn't in the judge's courtroom
Ten minutes and she wants to see my lawyer
in her chambers. Anxiety trying to take my
freedom. Ineffective counsel on this case.
It's time to fire my lawyer
for failure to disclose information.
Sometimes I think he is working with
the District Attorney. I have to take that
risk and believe I won't be held in contempt.
Court Officials know what I am saying is true.
I can't justify their bullshit!

ONE HARD PRICK SUPER-SIZED

I boarded an iron horse.
The downtown express pulled off
and I was riding the EL.
This man parked his shit in the crack of my ass.
It was parked in me like a sardine.
His bulge filled up my ass.
He rode me in locomotion.
Just as the train pulled in,
I could feel a sexually explicit nut . . .
the door opened and the man was gone . . .
He came on me downtown,
and I'm still going uptown.
My ass is wet from the bulge.
ONE HARD PRICK SUPER-SIZED . . .

A DIME

This mother fucker
was picking up his dime
out of the street holding up traffic.
I yelled for him to hurry up
and the bastard pulled out a 9mm pistol.
Pointed it right at my face in broad daylight.
Nervous and scared, I looked closer.
It was my little cousin.
I said "Desi, that you?"
He panicked and shot me by mistake.
DAMN, if I died,
it would have been
an accidental death in his mind.
My Benz has bullet holes.
I'm shell shocked and mad.
All I could do was jump out my car
and beat the shit out of him.
I never thought a dime could start a crime.

LIVING IN A HELL HOLE

Exploring alternatives
with insufficient funds.
To live in a hellhole.
Obligation to my family and myself.
Rats on the left of me.
Roaches on the right of me.
My infested hellhole!
This is not an acceptable lifestyle.
There's a need to divert
anger to management, my slumlord.
Life in a cold
damn drafty renovated garbage dump.
Agenda to escape this hellhole.
"HONEY I'M HOME"
Reluctant to admit.
I'm poor and I can't afford to move!

HIT BY A TRAIN

You were hit by a train.
Your iron horse pulled in a long time ago.
Our task to face your death.
Anticipation not knowing
very much about the mystery.
After the funeral,
you went to live in the house of gold.
Bereavement period
while reading the obituary
on the way to the cemetery.
Now you lay 6 feet under,
your soul still at rest in heaven.
Opportunity to come back to life after death.
A no brainer. Nothing left to think about.
For now, you lay down at peace.
Leaving me here with your heart in my chest,
and your thoughts in my mind.
"REST EASY MY FRIEND ..."

CAKE WAS THE SEXUAL PREFERENCE

Gravitating towards me.
Your sexual preference was cake.
While measuring my strengths,
You want my asshole.
Don't Think So!
Your perspective of love making
takes the cake.
Contribution to your masculinity.
Romance and scandal excited me too.
Sexual preference was emancipated. You see I am a minor.
You just popped my cherry. It hurt and felt good.
Journey elevated to another level.
                    MASTURBATION!
Handle your business baby.
My moms don't eat cake.
She wants a piece of your ass in court.
            YOU VIOLATED!
It would have been better if you preferred someone a little older . . .

IN MY CAR

Living in my car. All I see is stars.
The night is cold. Like the food I stole.
I lost my job and I've been robbed of my dignity.
Trying to hang on to my future.
I went to the hiring hall,
and I was forced to stand tall.
I waited on line only to find, it was a waste of time.
Skated 15 years in the work force
on a high school diploma.
That's no good anymore.
My life is in a coma.
College kids were hired, I'm fired.
My intelligence and experience
wasn't good enough.
Family disgraced
the shelter we'll face because my car's been towed away
and we have nowhere to stay.
Me and my family will continue to pray . . .

EBT FOOD STAMP BENEFIT CARD

Yes, you wanted to be my welfare pimp.
You didn't love me like you loved my
food stamps.
I knew that when you asked me
if you could leave some clothes
in my apartment.
I guess you want me to be your bootee call.
I question your motives about your clothing.
Would drugs or a gun be inside your clothes bag?
I was wondering
if you were rolling like that now.
You need to take your clothes
and keep them in wifey's house.
She's your headache,
the backstabbing whore.
Don't ask to live in my house.
I'm not letting you cock block up in my crib.
It's enough I'm selling my ass
for you in the street.
That's all my relationship
with you is about.
I need the extra money
to support my family.
Selling my body
kept me in the clinic.
Being a lady of the night
is my outside job.
Hustling to gain cash money
to go along with my food stamps.
Let's not get our relationship twisted.
I'm classy, you're trashy! FOOD STAMPS
Satisfaction guaranteed not anymore.

I have an E. B. T. Food Stamp Benefit Card.
To go with my tramp stamp!
You don't have to hunt me down at
the check cashing place anymore.
Your begging escalated since
welfare cheese.
Your belly full
And
You're still taking bull.
Stop waiting on my public assistance.
I'm not surviving off your thug love.
You keep telling me how if I let you get,
$100.00 off my food stamp benefit card,
You'll give me $70.00 in cash money.
I can't let you hustle me out of my food money.
So don't look for me to sell my food stamps.
You're looking for total self satisfaction.
I'm looking for self gratification . . .

TO LOOK AFTER YOU

God embraced
me
with open
arms.
A comfort of reinsurance.
A beautiful moment.
His spirit nurtured my soul.
"Lord," I spoke out to him.
"I love you too."
My heavenly father
gave
me
the strength to
look after you!

MR. TIGHT ASS

A mutual acquaintance said
he wanted to make love to me.
He also stated he'd take
care of me financially.
He was looking for someone to love.
He pulled out a strap on and
said he wanted to strap it on me.
Mr. Tight Ass wanted to get
boned and needed my
assistance. I could not believe,
     Mr. Tight Ass.
Wanted to strap a penis on me.
A female who is strictly dickly.
He wants me to pleasure him
by dominating the situation
So he could act out
his sexual exploitations
by spreading his cheeks.
I will not compromise myself
in his sexual exploitations.
He wanted a dick in his ass.
My spirit wasn't lifted,
but his ass was his last
sweet heart was a fudge packer.
I told my brother about Mr. Tight Ass.
He said his name on the
street is Daddy Blow Pop.
He polished all the fellas off.
He's known for giving good head.
I guess he's blowing up.
It's time for him to open wide.
He sounds like a real ass lick.

BUY OUT

I'm taking the buy out.
Justice the American way.
Different rules for different nationalities.
Ignoring my rights!
Living bigotry sometimes,
Grants me immunity from the
rules and regulations.
You can't break me.
So, cut the drama.
Can't I plea bargain my color
for a lighter sentence.
I have lived by the law.
My money says "in God we trust."
Who's trusting me.
I don't feel it.
I take the fifth on economy issues.
I like my independence and having a job.
I'd rather take the buy out
and become self-employed.
So, I'm taking the buy out.
I will not buy into the bullshit.
I am economically depressed . . .

G. I. JERK

G. I. Jerk
Bust a nut and now he's gone.
A regular G. I. Jerk
my American hero.
When he comes back from his mission,
it's on and poppin' sexually.
Oh I forgot, he can't accept phone calls.
He's married, were creeping.
Pussy on fire,
hadn't had any since October.
Now that I had the dick,
I know I like the rest of the package.
It can't finish like this,
a vulnerable moment for me.
He fucked my head up.
DAMN . . .

HUMAN CLONES

Unable to adopt!
Don't have no one to be your baby daddy.
Imagine,
human clones in the ghetto.
Is this biologically right?
To fix what we feel should be fixed?
"CLONING IN THE GHETTO"
Advertised in yesterday's newspaper.
Clone babies
a duplication of what already exists.
Now available
to the poor and middle class!
Birth from a sales man.
Question:
is this federally or privately funded?
I do pay $140.00 a month
on a Medicaid spend down.
God's child
a new creation of life
on the market for sale.
Will my child be tax deductible?
Cloning—vs.—Birth
with sex.

It's time to challenge medical ethics.
What dilemmas does the child face?
Does retardation play a part
of this human intelligence?
Will this child
be born with disastrous diseases?
Is cloning babies immoral?
Looks, cries and shits
the same as all other babies.
Even bleeds the same.
Do you really know what they are recreating?
What will be put on childbirth records?
HUMAN CLONE ~~ GOD'S CHILD!

FINE-ASS MOTHERFUCKER

White lace satin sheets,
dotted his I's
was always neat.
Perfect smile
grinned ear to ear.
While standing tall
so I could hear.
The jealous bitches
who I didn't fear.
Bustier tops with
thongs to match.
The knight on the white horse
should be my catch.
THAT FINE-ASS MOTHERFUCKER
was always my pick.
Every time I turned around,
He'd act like a prick.

HONORED

Honored by his presence,
graced by his inner strength,
such a warm feeling.
Got my doubts about loving him.
This is a decent man.
I'm pampered,
while he comforts me.
Challenged by his sex drive and lots of romance.
It's inevitable we'd be together.
He's given me hope on life.
I feel he'll do right by me.
While drinking Crystal,
he had entertained the thought of marriage. Then,
he starts an argument,
revealing the fact I lied.
When I met him, I stated
"I was a virgin!!"
I'm in shock that he'd be belittling me.
An impact to my heart.
The whole argument is an outrage!
I'm trying to keep my spirits up.
So I can be in a good place in my life.
Through his closing argument,
My current perception
of the relationship has changed.
I'd be honored to try to keep this decent man,
but now I know.
I can't be wrong
And
strong at the same time.
I LIED . . . Sympathy not required!

RUNNING AROUND

Running around
with the other woman.
I'm glorifying your bullshit.
While you try to fuck me without grease.
My cheating husband.
Only thing we really established
is the fact we have kids together.
Dope running you and
your friends around in circles.
"IT'S LIKE SHIT, FOLLOWING SHIT" ... Genocide!
Your dad
treated your mom
the same way.
Now he's a nocturnal crack head.
History has taught me that
this part of life is immoral.
This has to stop ...

A BOOK BONUS COLLECTION

ONE-DOZEN
STORYTELLING POEMS

BY
La'Rahz ~ R.E.O.I.

POEMS FROM HER PAST ACCOMPLISHED WORK

TO THANK READERS

FOR THEIR SUPPORT WHILE COMPLETING

"A KINGDOM OF CONTROVERSY"

Thank you so much . . .

THE BONUS BEGINS: THE FETUS

The fetus is here, and
you're fucking another.
What will the fetus become?
Will I be a mother?
My mind in despair
'cause the fetus is here.
Your Johnson about
a baby in doubt.
Obsessed with your new bitch,
not the fetus you ditched.
Oops, I forgot you said she was rich.
Not even a chance for a dad,
like you had.
Abortion in progress, and
you're already glad.
The decision made without fetus,
constitutional right,
and that's only because
my budget is tight.
Death sentence before birth.
Operation at dawn.
The thought of a baby,
The history is gone.

DRIVEN

Driven with passion,
beat in my heart,
steady I lay,
penetration deep.
Sliding in further,
your shit still erect,
wetness,
pleasure I did not expect.
Warm hands caressing my body,
Dick wet,
Nipples stood up firmly.
When tongue touched
My breast.
Lay your pipe, baby,
long,
dick me real good.
Fulfill me with pleasure,
as long as you could.

La'Rahz - Roslyn O'Flaherty Isaacs

GOD'S CHILD

God's child,
off to war.
thou shall not kill,
bill of rights
from the devil,
bombs, guns, casualties, and body bags,
wars, lost mind and souls
families distorted,
unpaid bills left behind,
bended truths,
wars, billion dollar rate,
making
single-parent households
ruined, damaged.
Who has the right to play
God and send
God's child to war.
The father of our country
versus
Our Father, who art in heaven.
The thought of all this
just blows me away . . .

TO BE THE PEOPLE

We have the right
to be the people,
but it just doesn't seem
to be that way.
All the minds have
gone astray
to the man who corrupted
our minds and our souls,
and left the white powder
and dust to hold.
It will hold your soul.
It will make you old.
You'll find yourself real
Bitter and cold
when
the money runs out
and the clout
is gone,
there'll be plenty of time
to weep and mourn.

La'Rahz - Roslyn O'Flaherty Isaacs

MISTER CHEEBA MAN

Mister Cheeba Man,
nickel bag on the corner,
seeds burning my clothes.
E-Z Wider, Bamboo.
Just one sheet for morning
spliff, joint made from roaches.
Now I have a buzz.
I run into a pothead
inviting me to smoke a
blunt.
Umm, ganja,
puff, puff, pass
tokes of grass
smell of fonta leaf
that I had stashed.
Phillie, White Owl,
Chocolate smoke.
Smoked a whooler
was no joke.
The herb and crack,
it was great.
I'm mellow now.
This wasn't fate.

YOU PICKED YOUR FRUIT

You picked your fruit,
so watery and ripe.
I never thought
I'd be your type.
The delight is here
for you to see,
I'll sit awhile
around your G.
The cherry is ready
for you to split;
you prefer
to suck my tit.
My cherry got hot,
just like jubilee,
all moist and wet
for you to get.
I know it's the best
Thing you've had yet.

ON VACATION

On vacation.
You liar.
Your prick
I caught out.
That lady,
she sucked it
as you swung it about.
Cum in her mouth,
her legs spread.
No doubt,
And
you're walking around
me and think you have clout.
The clout is gone.
The condom is torn.
Nine months later,
your baby is born.
Vacation is over,
your dick is dead.
We don't even have
money to buy any bread.

I AIN'T GOT NO CRACK

I ain't got no crack.
I cooked my coke
all in my pipe.
I puffed and puffed
with all my might.
The sight I seen,
The rush was mean,
The chip of ice
That burned:
I yearned for another puff.
Can't get rid of this stuff.
Coke, Smoke, tears,
I choked.
Have no money,
and I'm still broke.
I want some more.
I know for sure,
that will be the only cure.
My cravin' is here,
It's time for more.
I can't afford to pass
the door . . .

YOUR MOTHER

She's your mother,
She's not mine,
Yet, you feel I
should kiss her behind.
I spread my legs
like she spreads hers,
but I should listen
to her nasty slurs?
She tries to tell
me what to do,
sometimes I wonder
if she's screwing you too.
If she continues
to act like this,
it will only
make
me pissed.
So if you don't stop her,
I know I will.
I think you better ask,
your mother to chill.

ULTIMATE TRUTH

Ultimate truth
or
false allegations?
Investigator, prosecutor, judge,
criminal theory of the law.
Hearings, discussing,
Legal status of the case.
Self-esteem low,
making me lose faith
in my lawyer.
Trail on plea bargain gone.
Now I'm in jail, awaiting trial,
All shanked up,
not even a smile.
The beating I took,
officers corrupt.
They jigged me and kicked me
because I wouldn't
shut up.
Thoughts of suicide,
but I have too much pride.
Time to thank Jesus.
God's still on my side.

MEN RISING UP

Men rising up,
fighting for their lives.
Order in the court,
provides a verdict of
guilty or not guilty.
Media real heavy.
Court surrounded by
national guards
who have killed people
without reasonable doubt;
why aren't they on trail?
Is this justifiable homicide?
Are guards making a mockery
of the courts?
For this was
senseless killing
with no feeling of remorse.
For in guards' lives,
this is the norm,
court is adjourned.
Why are there different opinions
between men's norms and
guards' norms?
Next court date,
men fight for their lives
vs.
plaintiff,
but a stronger case is needed.
Establishment trying to
destroy them.

Dispute about
a lot of theories to many
hypothetical situations
even causing a mistrial.
Trial sabotaged,
testimony by plaintiff
no good,
so case
dismissed,
not
adjourned.

CYBER SEX

Internet.
Cyber sex.
Laying in your drawers
content.
Fantasizing,
craving it,
a climax.
The thought of penetration,
foreplay,
it's counterfeit sex.
Defusing the situation
by disrobing on screen,
the talk of your penis,
the heads that she's seen.
You open your hands
and your pecker came out,
then got on your knees
and swung it about.
Her pussy
was ready,
all wet,
no doubt.
You rubbed
on your johnson
to show her your cream,
her mouth flew open,
and you started to dream.
A vision of cunt placed in your face,
now your mouth was open and ready to taste.

THE BONUS

12-PACK
OF
STORYTELLING
ENDS . . .

BEAUTIFIED

*I dream of perfection. I'm a man
with female body parts. I just want
to be beautified. I'm trapped in a
fucked up face. My appearance,
identity and behavior is not a
gender norm. Morally unattractive
by my appearance. My worse
nightmare is an obsession. That I
have to be beautified. I'm a cross
dressing transgender. Changing
body parts. My plastic surgery
cost me at least, two hundred
and fifty thousand dollars or more.
My obsession with procedures has
me addicted to pain killers. I am
an addict and a manipulator for
prescription drugs for pain.
I started out with 800mg
of Motrin. I love taking
Oxycotin and being hospitalized
to get morphine. Prescription
intervention needed. I'm fighting
the addiction against myself.
I had breast and calf implants.
The surgery on my face caused
me to be scared and disfigured.
I put collagen in my lips. I thought
I needed this filler. The extreme
transformation of cosmetic surgery
caused infections.
The doctors were board certified.
I never thought I would turn out
ugly. I pressured myself to look
perfect. It was an obsession. I
was an addict to plastic surgery.*

Life is one big ball of confusion.
My external appearance and
complication was a horrible
night mare. My body disorder
made me question, did I really
need an image make over. Broke
still in dept to medical specialist.
I couldn't stop wanting to be
beautified. My Adam's apple was
removed! I'm waiting for surgery.
To fix new scares. I want to fix my
far head, nose and eyebrows. A
laser was used to remover my
facial hairs. I am mortified about
my disfigured body parts.
I need money so I can be
        beautified!
This has been a real hormonal
experience. I don't need the
homophobia that I have endured
from some people in my life.
It doesn't seem fear to me. I
thought I would be socially
acceptable. I just need to be
beautified.
        So I can be a Princess!
I decided to go shopping to buy
some new clothes. I could not
find anything on 3$^{rd(BX)}$ avenue.
So I went to 125th street. I got out
the cab 125th and Lenox Avenue.
I walked to the corner and saw
my mother. She did not know
who I was. She had not seen me
in years. I said hello mother! She
looked at me and had to take a
2nd glance. She was in shock. At
my appearance and what I looked

like. She grabbed me and hugged me.
Screamed my name Majhar, Majhar,
my baby! She cried tears of joy. We
talked she said, she prayed every
night. For the Lord to keep me safe.
She was glad, her prayers were
answered. I explained to my mother
that before my operation. I thought
that genetic testing could tell me why
I was stuck between being a male and
female. Now that I have a Mangina.
I fight with myself sometimes, because
I have changed God's image. When I
had my sex change surgery. Now
I have female reproductive parts.
I lived as a woman for a year before
I had my operation. It bothers me
that I can't have a baby. I fight with
the fact, that I can't have children of
my own. I need parental love from
you Ma. Dad has disowned me.
I'm having trouble finding a place
in society. It's like I don't have civil
rights or human rights. Is religion
the law for transsexuals? Religious
leaders made me feel. That my life
as a transsexual is the beginning of
hell. Well I'm glad I still have you Ma.
That keeps me from being depressed. I
am not suicidal. I can't understand my life.
Who will rescue my heart and soul. Who
will accept the decision I have made for
myself besides you Ma. My mom said
we were all made in God's image. So I
was beautified at birth. I must love what
God gave me and believe, I am beautiful
in mind and spirit. I must not live in shame.
After me and Mama's talk. I decided I have

to 360 the self pity. Revaluate my thinking
and live in the now. Before I get depressed
to the point. Where I want to kill myself. I
don't want to be on anti depressant anymore.
Society can be so cruel sometimes.

"Mama says I'm an expression of Love"
If I pray, I will be set free by the Hands of the Lord!!!

HAVE YOU HEARD?

Have you heard? My dad
Relocated to another women's
bed. My maternal protection is
my mother. My grandmother is
my stability. My environment
has changed. I'm nervous, will
I survive this situation.
Grandma says, it can only make
me stronger. Don't be discouraged
with faith, wisdom will come. My
parents are divorced, it's emotional.
My heart is scarred, my brain in a
trance.

GO FIGURE!

My father a subordinate male.
Possessed by another woman's
authority. Who is just a new
piece of ass.
My mother's marriage is
damaged, finished. She
can't believe the trust in
her marriage had been
betrayed. I have not
forgiven my mother and
father, for how I was
raised. Fault finding
their business with my
opinions. Making their
mistakes and situations
the reason why? I am
the way I am. My friend
Julia told me I better
thank God my mother
and father were stupid
enough to birth my ass.

I could have been aborted.
My up bringing, was what
it was.
Julia thinks I'm selfish,
spoiled and a self
centered human being.
                    DRAMA, DRAMA, DRAMA!
Julia says I should not
make my parents
mistakes all about me.
What I speak is not
constructive criticism.
It's resentment with a
silver lining. I could
never fit in their shoes so
I should not try to wear
them. Everyone is subject
to mistakes. They don't
need to be subjected to my
approval or control.
{parent abuse}
It's not necessary to be
verbally abusive.
They can't keep being a self
destructive victim. How can
I process the fact. That all
this confusion is really my
problem. It's time I admit it
and find out, what my parents
can do to help me. To continue
to keep living the same drama
over and over is psychotic behavior.
I run around looking for world
pity. I must take the blame for
my mistakes. It's time I own
up to them and stop blaming
everyone else!
My emergency is not their

*emergency. Mama always
says family takes care of
family no matter what.
She instilled in us that we
must not take life or people
for granted. Positive love
and courage will help you
over negative situations.
Mama said I will come to
peace with myself if I free my
heart and mind from all my
trouble. She feels I have
selective anxiety that's
defensible by any objective
reasoning . . . Mama trying to
make me understand that she
doesn't define who I am as a
person!*

SUBSTITUTING

He exploded
a sexual
moment.
We shared multiple
orgasms without a
argument. Maybe I should
trick him and give him a baby.
Maybe the off spring will
make everything better and
help fulfill my aching heart.
Just the thought of tricking him
is making my conscious feel better.
Substituting a fetus for a beating
or verbal abuse. I was living in an
distrustful relationship. I thought the
abuse would stop.
I let him pump a baby inside of
me. Hoping he would marry me.
My plan didn't work he is still my
man whore. As my belly rose we
had new family quarrels. He would
slap me from time to time. The
verbal abuse continued. This illicit
love was not healthy. He complained
always saying I could not cook or
clean. He says all women are good
for is making babies. Never giving me
credit for the stability that I bring to
my family. I hardly ever see him.
He stays drunk all the time. Since I
had the baby he won't work anymore.
I will be raising my family with
him or without him. This is a
dysfunctional family. Talk
about the beginning of a

relationship, being just like
the end. Well I think it's
*time to dead this shit**!!!***
What I am experiencing is
not healthy for my child.
I can't continue to live in a
battered lifestyle. He will
not continue to provoke me.
The drama is killing me.

MY BOILER MAKER

When I stepped in the bar.
I thought I was a star. A
date rape drug and alcohol,
was my boiler maker. It
invaded my space with no
evidence, no trace.
FLASH—CAMERA—ACTION!!!
I felt high in a daze. My legs were
wide open as the people gazed.
    Go head with that bull shit!
I thought in my mind. As the camera
took pictures. Of my most private
body parts. Disrespected, I felt raped
by a camera, alcohol, and drugs.
Traumatized from not knowing the
unwanted people. That stayed in my head.
How could they be so anal?
Bodies with know faces. It's time to
wake up. For now I'm alone. I don't
even remember. How I got home.
This dirty little secret. It still haunts
my soul. Who can I tell? I can't figure
it out. An impact of lawlessness. How
can I fight back? Where do I start from?
My legs they did spread. I guess, I
should thank God. That I am not dead!

FATAL DESTINY

My difficulties over the years has been
food and more food. My husband keeps
feeding my nervous energy. Thinking
he's keeping me fed well. He loves thick
women. I devour a over abundance of
food. Causing a misfortune to my body. I
had one heart attack. Food ruing my
health. Rolls of fat on my stomach. I
can't even bend down and tie my shoe.
Cellulite on my legs. Lumpy fat on my
buttocks. Obesity the ultimate out come
to my over eating. My health is fraught
with constant danger. Obesity making
my life peril to destruction. This should
not be my fatal destiny. My husband
calls me fatty too much. For being a big
woman. His cruel insults and putting me
down. Doesn't allow the food to settle,
my mind or my nerves anymore. I now
have to decrease my calories and
start exercising. I hope our meditation
counselor will help stop the disputes, me
and my husband has over my eating
disorder. I need to lets go of my stress.
It's time to slow down on this weight gain.
I need to start eating fruit, vegetables and
fish. I hope exercise will release a lot of
my stress. Food an my trash talking
husband won't be my incurable destiny.
I guess I've taken one bite to many.
I can't let him bend my ass out of shape!

MASQUERADE MARRIAGE

I'm living a marriage of sex and lies.
My husband is a playa without a
condom. He could never control
his erection. The condition of this
marriage, fucked my head up.
My husbands, home wrecker is
a fucking whore a real belligerent
bitch. She invaded the premises
of my home and slept in our bed.
A sacred area, which he allowed
her to surrender her pussy. He
impregnated us both at the same
time. Now he states he doesn't
love me anymore. He said me
and his fling should have had a
three some with him. It could
have saved him the time of
sneaking around. He said,
all him and his whore were
doing was a lot of fucking
and sucking!
How could he talk to me like
this? After he took me on a
long journey, with his little
wee wee.
My marriage is now hopeless
and ruined. Our baby is due
and I don't understand. Which
direction our masquerade
marriage is headed. I understand
that babies are Gods blessing.
Spiritually pure and blessed with
holy love. For me to attain love
and hope in this marriage again.
It would take a lot of compassion

and sympathy. I have a lot of
misguided hatred built up inside
of me. I'm contemplating violence
that doesn't have to occur. I won't
continue to live in this masquerade
marriage. I no that all this irrational,
negative energy can't evade my
space anymore. He has to be done
with, this bitch ass whore. He claims
he's through with her.
He states he only sees her to maintain
a relationship with his child. Yet he can't
sit still long enough to provide love or
comfort in our home for me and our newborn.
All he is really offering me is life full of shame.
I am struggling in his sins. He's
just inconsiderate, with a non
caring attitude. There was a time
in my life when I thought this man
was the answer to my prays. The
truth is all I have is a masquerade
marriage! I am grateful for the fact
that I have learned how to raise my
child alone. I have become quite
proficient at it. My child loves me
unconditionally.

FIGHTING TO MAKE A CHANGE

I question if my identity has been
taken away. I feel like I'm about to
face a life sentence. I'm about to
become a victim of circumstances.
Economics have been taken away.
Making me emotionally and financially
drained. I watch the destruction and
the division of my neighborhood.
The feeling of being oppressed is
causing distress to others. America
the land of opportunity. I feel like I'm
living in a third world country. People
are looking for leadership. To make
a difference, I sit and watch the
complexity in peoples influenced
behavior. Competent individuals are
feeling inadequate and not attentive.
To the fight to make a change. Yet
they know the importance of civility.
As they watch people being pushed,
out of the job market. Children's education
are being threatened. Schools are being
closed. Medical conditions are
compromising people's health. I
see freedom cost. It is the commonality
for people to find their way. A foundation
is needed as we walk with integrity. Lack
of understanding our history. Makes us
repeat it. I applaud people who are
keeping a strong state of mind. As they
fight to make a change in this political
universe.

SANTA CLAUS

Santa Claus
big fat ass.
Why he let
my Christmas pass.
He left no gifts
for me to see.
Is this because
we had no tree.
I left milk and cookies.
So he could snack,
but he carried no
toys on his back.
Me and my family.
We didn't get jack _ _ _ _ !

A LIFE STYLE WITH A TESTIMONY, CAN YOU HEAR ME LORD?

Blessed, oh Lord
in thee
I
prayed.
For I feel I was singled out by
the devil. The devil has been
on my shoulders long enough.
Yet! I was living in a state of being.
An act of destruction. Lord I've
tried freedom and justice the
American way. City, State and
Federal legislation it doesn't help.
I've lost faith in the Constitution. I
have pledged allegiance to the flag.
Of my government and converted to
the national anthem. When I played
by the rules, intensity fighting
poverty. Pain in my soul as I try
to hold on to my innocence. I was
living off of thug love. Lord I am
not being blessed from hanging in
the hood. Now I lift my head in
shame. For I forgot how to pray!
Prophesying over myself with a
divine inspiration. People were
taking my kindness for weakness.
I helped everyone but myself.
Oh God comfort me as I bring the
mess that I have made and put it
in your hands. I was lost in life's
tragedies. I became an abused
house wife. Lost my babies father
to the next woman. There was

interference, from in laws. They
were partial to one situation. "Their
child an individual with a sense of
entitlement". It's a challenge to
conceive this mental image of family.
In laws not of blood existence. This is
a conflict of interest. This is disruptive
to my mind. While I suffer oppressed
elements of abuse. My hearts tired of
being on the defense. The final
destination is not all gravy.
When you're being treated in a
condescending way. A marriage
of lies, power, manipulation and
control. Forced to live the unknown.
An emotional impact with reference
to negative characteristic's. Living
through events of theory for reasoning.
How could this go on without anyone
noticing. I have stolen to feed my
kids. I forgot how to praise them and
tell them I love them. Recreation drugs
used to medicate myself, to save my mind.
Encountered a sexual transmitted
disease. As I looked for love from my
spouse. Love caused an abortion. The
loss of life rejected as an embryo. Born
to suffering a damaged soul. Retired
from the work force. Put out pasture on
disability. Tragedies have touched my
soul. I lost my mind living, to survive in
the system. My diverse corrupt mind
needs healing. As I live in my incomplete
cycle of life. I lost my comprehension of
the Lords' word. I was a product of my
environment. I prayed for progress
beyond the life I lived.
I know now man cannot help me.

I must not rely on man. I can only
rely on God. I sold my soul to the
devil and bit the bullet of deception.
This is irrelevant to, the love of
God? My prognosis it's time to
engage, in the house of the Lord.
I stand before you Jesus son of
God and ask you to advise me.
Will the truth inspire, me to take
responsibility For my actions, as I
gain wisdom? Lord lift me up from
this wickedness. Heal me from my
troubles. Tension is arising. Put
me on my feet. So I can endure my
distress and misfortunes. My ideology,
of life deteriorates from my soul. It has
made me less than a full human being.
I cannot continue to live in damnation,
angry and upset. A whole complete
cycle of action, living on the edge. I
must be free from drama. Lift this
burden in which I carry. Keep me from
perpetuating feelings that causes
problems. Bring closure Lord Jesus to
my altercation. For slippage always
keeps me from my dreams. Support
me as I put trust in you. I pray for a
safe space. For you to assist me in
seeking your ministry. I must be
free in Gods family. So I pray to the
almighty God to delivers me from
lusting in the devils temptation.
Give me strength and faith to be
able to forgive others. Give me the
power to regain my compassion for
people's misfortunes. For I am
ready to pray. I want to represent
the Lord Jesus. Patterns of my past did

La'Rahz - Roslyn O'Flaherty Isaacs

not allow me to serve God. I need to be
the boss of my life. For now, it's time for
me to return to my roots. In the faith of
God's word. I have taken into consideration.
That the streets were waiting for me. Drama
has unfolded in my life. I want to come in
control with my demons. Making my life
valuable and rewarding in a full circle.
A rational bond between me and
Jesus is needed. So he can teach me
the simplicity of living freedom from
complexity. I must not be an idol I my
own mind. I'm trying to live a stress
free life.
Restricted from pain and everyone's
nonsense. My life is just an unpredictable
roller coaster.   Life won't kill me Lord. I'm tired
                    of living a destructive lifestyle!
                    God I know you're listening.
                    God I'm glad your still
                        working on me,
                        till I get it right.
So I say, thank you Lord.
For letting me lay my burden before
you. As I live through my mistakes.
I appreciate the favors that I have
endured in my life.
"Father you are worthy to be praised."
A spiritual place within me believes in:
1 SAMUEL CHAPTER 16—VERSE 7 SAYS,
"But the Lord said unto Sam-u-el,
look not on His countenance, or on the height of His stature
because I have refused Him: for the Lord seeth
not like man seeth; for man looks on the outward
appearance, but the Lord looketh on the heart."

IF I DIE

Your mother ages gracefully. As your
brother suffers with an aids related illness.
Family spirit inadvertently shares the
thought of losing him. He dares not
dwell in self pity. He pulls family closer
together. Teaching his gender bender
experiences. Which he learned when
he was exposed to the drug culture.
The family was confused. When He
stated "if I die at least I lived a full life"
QUESTION! Did he really live or patronize
what he had been exposed to.
The family never understood the
consequences. That led to his death . . .
They loved and enjoyed him. Until the
Lord received him, so that he could rest.

PLAYA

So you want to be a playa.
Well playa, I'm tired of
glorifying the bull shit.
Love fulfillment gone,
i'm over whelmed in
preexisting condition
of brutal beatings.
Which I consider a hate crime.
You have no conscious.
Domestic disputes not my
styles. A empowerment that
restricts me from family and
friends. Why do I allow and
enabled you to keep me
hostage? Stalking me
because you don't want to
let me go. You don't own
me. Threatening to ride a
train on me with your home
boys. You annoy me with
your lies, bull shit and
manipulation. I don't fear
your personality. So don't
get it twisted. I remember
when I wanted to bring you
home and bring the man out
of you. Wiping your tears,
while fighting for positive
growth. This should have
been an outlet to chill with
a bit of sun shine. I thought
we would live, life without
pain. This life is not for me.
I don't know where our lives
are headed. Connected in

confusion in this low income
life of misery. Circumstances
have changed, our cordial and
discreet sexual relationships is
over. I have had a tough
defense through your bull shit.
This is the final episode, of you and
your sexual exploitations with the
other women your fucking.
I'M TIRED
OF GETTING PLAYED
PLAYA.
GO PLAY WITH YOURSELF . . .

AUTHORITY CRIMINAL MINDED

Falsified unethical, criminal minded
authorities says it's my last days in
society. Turn myself in Monday
morning. Assaults my verdict.
Stealing should be my crime. I
turned myself in pleaded guilty.
Looking for a lighter sentence.
Fuck my integrity. Convicted by
law, arrested and jailed how tacky.
Imprisoned with an illegal deal.
Immorality! Now I'm a prisoner 3rd
time offender. Implicated by false
allegations. I need help from
those who govern our country.
Until this happens, I must stay focused
and live what is happening now.

I AIN'T FUCKING WITH YOU

I can't believe this Mother Fucker
pushed up on me like that. The ass
hole is straight up 7-30. I can't fuck
with him. I HAD TO FLIP ON HIM . . .
He's scandalous! I let him know your
money's short. I don't care how much
you're holding in your draws. Evidently
what you don't have is a conscious.
The thing that kills me is. Even though
your dick is as hard as a chicken bone.
It's no bigger than my thumb . . .
I question if you can, go hard and bring it!!!
Because you walk like,
your nuts are stuck up your ass!!!
That's another reason.
I AIN'T FUCKIN' WITH YOU!

PEDOPHILE ON VIAGRA

*Old ass pedophile. Allowed to
live next door. Went to jail for
rape. He was released in less
than 8 years. He is a welfare
recipient. Sexual aggressive
person brought Viagra with his
government funds. This should
be a federal offense. His name
and identification is not on the
sex offender's registry. I could
not believe there was no
registration on his sexual past.
I was lured through pity—pat rape.
Seduced and totally violated. He
said I excited him as he chocked
me. I was black and blue. I almost
pasted out as I was sexually touched
orally. This is a pedophile with no code of
conduct. I prayed he had a vasectomy. I
am a child, not a sexual provocative
person. My mind was destroyed by this
pedophile. Molested—raped, yes I
was penetrated by a pedophile. Whose
penis was able to get an erection from
Viagra. His prescription should have
never been filled. A pedophile that gets
Money, Food Stamps and Medicaid.
Government aid with his Viagra. This
violent act is a serious crime. He should
not get anymore help from Viagra. It's
crazy how Mr. Pedophile can afford an
erection. I may as well been fucked by the
government!!!*

DOLLARS AND CENTS

Dollars and cents,
use to pay rent.
I have
to stop eviction,
that doesn't
make sense.
The late fee
was doubled,
cause the white powder.
Is extorting money from
me.
Brain now on empty,
fried to a crisp.
Don't have any food
to put in kids dish.
My man is ecstatic
and drugs won't give up.
I'm functioning under
its guide lines.
My mind is corrupt.
Hearts pumping fast,
my life is a mess.
I have a sudden
pain in my chest.
Screaming and hollering.
I feel like a fool.
I'm out of control.
My soul I will lose.

ICE, ICE CRAZY

Meth.
Cooking in the basement,
factory!
Determining my future.
Hitting that glass pipe.
Watching it burn.
CRYSTAL METH . . .
You've been my head ache for years.
Annoying me, feeding on my human misery.

To Escape Crystal . . .

The chase is on while looking for
the first encounter. I owe money
and sexual favors. Revelation
with no judgment. Three or four
times a day I shoot up.
My level of spirit,
has gone to the devil.
OH
My crystal meth, your
treating me bad. I've
been up one week straight.
Drugs talking to me,
telling me to use.
Chemical dependency
I can't stop.
ICE ICE CRYSTAL!
Shut up
CRYSTAL!
I can't hear you.
Your driving me ice ice crazy.
It's a done deal.
The experience has been real!

S.O.S.

Girl Friend!
He doesn't care about you.
He only wants some duckets.
S. O. S
The smoke signals went up. Your
pimp keeps you so drugged up.
That you look like an old throw
back jersey. He beat you like
you stole something. Blacked
both your eyes yesterday.
You don't even have no
money. You acting like you
have an IQ of a twelve year old.
Now you're locked up scared. To
ask him to bail you out again.
This is not the time to be jailing.
It's a pity your pimps and johns,
seem so important to you. You
love them unconditionally.
You are betraying your family
and friends. Who are willing to
save you. Family members
can't believe. The trust you
have in your pimp.
Maybe you should consider
the source. In which your trust
is going to. He won't keep
you from self destruction.
Your pimp beat you near
death.
HOSPITALIZING YOU!
You stay in physical altercation.
Your Johns keep you in danger.
Raping your soul of its purity.
Now your forced against your

La'Rahz - Roslyn O'Flaherty Isaacs

*will. To be a prostitute and a
drug abuser. Escort services
making your prostitution legal.
A higher class of prostitution.
Clock that dollar baby. Your
Pimp is watching out for you.*

S. O. S.

*You were found dead for the
love of your pimp. Know one
can help you now. This was
the consequence of walking
the street.*

HOOD RAT

Neighbors near by calling you
a freak hoe. Just a straight up
slut from the hood. You allowed
guy to smash it. Sex drive out
of control, psychologically and
emotionally being disrespected.
drinking and drugging and
sleeping with various dudes.
They are all from the same
hood. The homies say they
hit that. They are calling you
a homie hopper you are
being sexually abused. If
you continue to be a hood rat.
Guess what the neighborhood
don't care about your VA Jay Jay.
I know you're tired of jumping
men's bones. Choose to be
healthy. You haven't had a
aids test in years. You can't
be happy with this insane life
style. Bondage while they
burned you with a cigarette.
Beat, raped and robbed of
your dignity. It's hard to let
yourself get into these guys
mentally. You know they
have a boner for you. They
just want to abuse your naked
body. I know this bothers you.
Admit to your emotions. They
didn't disappear.
Don't shut your eyes to their
psychotic hormones. Please
don't become a hood hopper.
The solution is to stop living,

the way that you are. Angry
and upset with the world.
People can only take
advantage of you. If you
associated with them and
allow it. This is a difficult
moment in your life.
Your vulnerable in the
hood. You need a spirit
of love. Don't look for comfort
and completion in a man.
Peace is your seed of love.
　　"Don't return evil with evil."
Exceed your expectation focus on
positive change that can get your
spirit right. Deal with your issues.
You will find strength within yourself.
Live what's truly within your heart
and head. Let your mind be free.
Don't let life consume you. You have
so much misery and regret bottled up
in you. It destroyed your confidence.
You're scared and tired of living in doubt.
Now you've become a quite soul. Your
reputation perceived you. Loose that
doubt, be optimistic. Truth and acceptance
for yourself will destroy, all the negative
obstacles in your way. Life with the right
perspective will help you exceed your
expectations. With a high spirit of self
confidence.
A month later you find out your
pregnant. You're trying to Guess
who the father is. Your Mama says
although she was not there for you.
She prayed for you everyday. She
knows her letters from jail empowered
you to live a more positive lifestyle.
Mama said I could be strong no matter
what the devil through my way. She

recognizes the anxiety in my unfamiliar
lifestyle. The continuation of abuse
and torture that I endured was mind
shattering an overwhelming. God told
her that I was safe. Mama's glad he
saved my sanity she said—
AMEN TO THAT!!!
Mama said I am a very intelligent
human being. Knowledge is essential
to advocate my survival skills. I have
book and street smarts to evaluate
my personal circumstances. I have to
contact the social worker in the hospital
to advocate the necessary resources for
my mental and physical health. All I have
to do is make it happen. I looked at her
like she was crazy. My moms just came
home from jail. This is the 3rd bid that I
have done with her. She is so self
absorbed within herself. I know her mind
is ready for self destruction. I didn't have
a normal childhood. Was this because of
her actions? Now she feels I should contact
a social worker.
When will I be able to contact my mother
emotionally, mentally and spiritually . . .
What gives her the right to tell me Amen?
This is a heart felt experience for me.
Look how long my moms has been in and
out of my life. Look how long I have been
abused. Why won't she address my issues?
I feel she feeding me a CROCK OF BULL.
Was this part of my destiny? Is this the price
I had to pay for her, to make amends with me?
I am devastated! I should not have, had to
endured this lifestyle.
My moms is opinionated and dismissive . . .
God will forgive my errors . . .
I feel God will definitely humble her spirit . . .
Amen!

BULLSHIT AND BUBBLE GUM

Stop talking to me about
your man. The way you
start a relationship. Is
how it's going to end.
Let that asshole know.
Everybody don't want,
bull shit and bubble gum.
He's chewing gum and
feeding you the bullshit.
HELLO!!!

BUBBLE GUM AND CANDY

Bubble gum and candy.
Memories and tears,
met and respected through
your travels as Aunty. You
were a glittering light. In my
gloomy room.
        WITH!
A curious wisdom. Fought
and fussed out of love. A
soul full of courage. We
were graced by your inner
strength. It was such a
warm feeling. You were
sent from above. Getting
gussied up to get dressed.
The finest clothes.
Your hearts on your sleeve.
Hair all done up who else,
can you please. Had time
to raise family. Like it was
a breeze. Your exuberant
life is just what you leave.

PEANUT BUTTER AND JAM

You were all over me like,
peanut butter and jam.
Trying to put it on me
while showing me your
circumcised.
WHAT'S THAT ABOUT!
Trash talking and straddling
me at the same time. Yeah!
I let you penetrate me. I have
something to tell you. I'm
doing your brother and I'm
not letting him go. Now you
want to keep the pussy, in
the family . . . Are you willing to
share. You're looking at me like.
The peanut butter is stuck. To
the top of your mouth and the
jam done changed to jelly.
"WHAT YOU CAN'T TALK!"

MY CHILD, MY ANGEL

My child,
My angel!
Is there a discrepancy? In what
path to take in life.
                    WHY?
You are a well rounded individual.
Don't put re-strengths on your
potential. That you just discovered.
Be thrilled not shocked. Understand
your fears, never worry.
The impossibilities will be displayed
before you. Bare witness to the fact,
that modesty will hold you back
                    sometimes.
Sometimes you sound tired of being
                    inspired.
DON'T BE!!!
Your blessed spread your wings.
        You have the energy,
     because you are my child.
        My angel light in my life.

MY BABY DADDY

You're not my father.
Just my baby daddy.
I am not answerable
to you.
You want me to call
you daddy. My father
is deceased. You say
you've changed well.
        NEWS FLASH!
People don't change.
They just mature.
Your ignorant ass,
just wants to act
        immature.
I can't wait for you to
mature. So I decided to
have desert with my entree.
You see I have matured.
You're not enough for me.
I'm cheating on you baby!
Know question about it.
I'm cheating and the desert
is good.

I'VE BEEN VIOLATED

I was brought up to think.
Family should love each
other. I should be able to trust
my family. My parents tried to
cover up the fact that I was
raped. By a family member
who had Penile Implant
Surgery. This assholes
Trojan. Natural rubber
latex caused me to have
an allergic reaction. Me
getting sick made my
parents confess that
abuse occurred. I'm
glad I was not his
fertile victim. There is
no justification for an individual
being sexually assaulted.
Aspiration and a desire to be
loved. Sent me in the arms of
my husband. Under false
pretense, he made me love
him. This man showed me he
was a real piece of shit . . .
        The bastards love departure.
        Was a tragedy to my misfortune!
A marriage full of anger,
agony and confusion.
Violation of my trust,
because of disastrous
events of my family.
I'm destined to be alone.
BUT I GOT THIS!

I can maintain.
I finally learned the violation
of my life. I was lonely within
myself. I don't need to be
anyone's wife. He should be
grateful to be in my life.

> *THIS WHOLE EXPERIENCE HAS*
> *TAUGHT ME, THAT I CAN'T LOVE*
ANYONE MORE THAN I LOVE MYSELF!!!

V. I. P.

PARTY TIME,
YES I AM V. I. P.
OF THIS PARTY
LET'S PARTY
YES I'M

            VERY. IMPORTANT. PUSSY.

V. I. P.
Yes they,
Brought it,
Tasted it,
Licked it,
Smelt it,
Screwed it,
Photographed it,
Finger fucked it and I'm still
V. I. P. pussy!

DOWN SOUTH DICK

Did you ever have
Dirty South Dick?
YES that D.S. DICK . . .
Thoughts of penetration
then straight down south
it goes every time.
One eye bandit.
Yes, bury your bone baby.
Brother hung so low with
great balls. Yes I want meat
with my stuff-in.
Dirty South loves to indulge in
a allude act. Weak moment
for my magnetized heart. His
wet tongue privilege opportunity.
A passionate splendid moment.
I enjoyed it when he licked,
deeper and deeper down.
Yes! His tongue knocked out
my clit. I loved that dirty Down
South dick. That how it was
when he went Down South
on me!!!

JOHNSON

Johnson
Don't like
Condoms,
Johnson
Likes
Sex.
If Johnson
Don't wear
Condom,
Johnson
Can just
Go play
Dead! I'm not a slobber.
I don't eat with my mouth open.
So Johnson will become Johnson
and Jerkson.
You can use your right hand
        for that.
STOP BEATING AROUND THE BUSH!
Oh, you aren't feeling that condom?
Guess Johnson isn't feeling aids
either.
YOU THINK FUCKING WITH A CONDOM
MAKES YOUR DICK GENERIC . . .
I GUESS WE'LL BE FUCKING GENERIC STYLE!

SEXUALLY ABUSED

Child sexually abused
by the hand of thy
father.
>   *NASTY!*
Daughter's a prostitute
and dad done brought
the pussy. Daddy says
she was his best fuck.
He wasn't even suppose
to sniff the twat. CHILD BORN OUT OF INCEST!
Baby's life is one big mess,
because daddy's parent and
grandparent of said child.
AIN'T THAT A MOTHERFUCKER.

BABY, YOU SPOILED ME LIKE THIS

BABY!
I can't deal with distance.
Bring your ass home. You
say you can't stand a weak
woman.
Questioning my survival skills.
Yes! You've become my safety
net. Controlling our destiny. I
married you for money and
security. You're putting your
manhood on a pedestal. Your
swagger isn't all that. Yet you
state this marriage is a tragedy.
for you. Now you need space
and distance. You've been gone
for one month.
Causing me an unhappy feeling
of uncertainty and doubt.
Baby it's time for you to come
home. You spoiled me like this.
My image is distorted and you
have become very judgmental.
Stating my body needs a quick
fix. You say I fell off and your
still doing me. My vitality and
beauty is lost. You call me the
ugly girl. Now I'm a morbid
obese person. You're critical
about my appearance. Saying
I'm addicted to food.
If you make me feel uncomfortable,
I have the right to make you feel
uncomfortable. Is this a noble
combination? The principles of
moral character.

What gives you the right
To regulate principles,
habits and requirements of others
disastrous misfortunes? Your sick
of finding onion rings and ding
dongs in the bed. I feel dissed
and dismissed. Cut me off some
slack. You're devastated about my
weight. Well baby, I'm a woman.
This is bigger better booty Baby.
You know it, that's why your still
hitting it. So you can't be truly
ashamed. Do right by me Baby.
The change can be good, so
help me. I feel hungry, I have to
eat . . . take your dick out the
pussy, you're hitting my guts.
Feed me Baby!

TIME TO SAY GOODBYE

I had my time to say goodbye.
Through a visit, phone calls and
memories. You have left, but
you'll never be distant from me.
For I have left the light on for you.
To create new boundaries for me
to follow. You showed me the way
to keep in touch with reality. All
I have to do is believe. For I will
search for the light for happiness.
In times of trouble, I am not afraid.
You showed me how to stay
away from deviant behavior. For
this I love you. I am ready to
start my life's journey with integrity.
Remember I can turn on the light
when ever necessary. I am saying
good-bye, but you'll never be left
in the dark.

La'Rahz - Roslyn O'Flaherty Isaacs

THIS ISN'T THE TIME TO JAIL

This isn't the time to jail.
The courts say I was
Presumed innocent on a
drug charge. A innocent
man should not have to cop out
to jail time. Especially when
he knows his shit is correct.
I've never been in trouble with the
law before. This is a invasion of
my life. I believe if someone
shows you who they are believe
it. The drugs were found on the
ground. There was nothing that
was presented in court that shows
I should have been handed this
unfavorable opinion. They had
no real evidence that the heroin
belonged to me. Well at least my
color didn't make me guilty. I
never personify people by color.
To speak a warning into my
future. Was like putting a knife in
my chest. My life was negotiated
for me, right in front of my face. A
conflict of interest to my freedom.
I should have the positive destiny,
that others see in me. My freedom
use to lie in my hands. I was released
in my own recognizance. Is this a
warning are they looking for, a second
occurrence to add on this court case.
The deferred prosecution proceeding
in my criminal case, will be put off
for a moment in time. I knew the court
officials were waiting for charges to

progressively get worse. I could not
believe I was living, under the
obligation of the courts conditions.
I'm praying that I hold up to societies
standards. Well if my ass gets in
trouble. I better be able to get out of
it. I realize if the conditions are met
my case may be dismissed. I can't
continue to live this life of politics.
I don't think courts stipulations will
be hard to abide by. I will be living
in damnation. I'm praying to God,
trouble doesn't follow me. I just
turned 18 years old and I don't
want to be incarcerated. Living in
a dorm with grown men. Men who
have nothing to lose. Men who
have been given a life sentence.
DAMN!!!
I was picked up in a stolen car.
Riding around with my man. In a
stolen Mercedes Benz. I didn't
realize the bitch was stolen. The
cops hand cuffed me and I was
thrown up against the car. To
make matters worse. The police
officer pulled a gun, from under
the seat where I was sitting.
My heart was pounding like I was
going to die. I started to wonder
was this gun used to kill anyone?
That's all I needed was to catch a
body. That would be a horrendous
case that I didn't need right about
now. Now I'm guilty by association.
I needed to see a lawyer.
My friend can't be my codefendant.
Our cases have to be split up. I only

asked home boy to give me a lift to
the Avenue, three blocks away. The
cops lifted my ass off to jail. When
I went to court. The judge didn't
even lift his head to look at me
when he made his decision.
I went straight to jail. Was I
considered a first time offender?
Will my charges be concurrent?
I didn't understand did the Judge
make a decision to run the cases
consecutively. I new that I would
be considered guilty. When it was
time to tell my side of the story.
God knows, I didn't no the car was
stolen. I didn't do anything wrong.
I kept telling the police officer that
the gun found under the seat.
wasn't mines. Me being let out on
my own recognizance's and then
picked up with Dude was not
suppose to happen, I'm still in shock
Dude had a rap sheet a mile long.
I had to speak to someone. I need a
lawyer! How could I be such an ass
hole? I just turned 18 years old two
days ago. My Moms upset with me,
right about now. She can't take the
fact her son was being accused of
being a dope dealer. My Mom said that
is just as bad as being a heroin addict.
I wasn't a junkie. I would never take a
ride on the white horse. I don't even
like needles. I could never see myself
having a habit with a itch. I can't blame
my mother for being mad. I can only
blame myself. All I wanted to do is
show my mother the man that she

raised. I let her down by promising.
I would stay out of trouble. I was
given a bullshit, legal aid lawyer.
My lawyer only came to visit me
one time. He is never in his office.
When I call his office he is always
in court. All this confusion is making
me lose faith in my lawyer. I am now
living with criminals. I'm not like them.
I have met men who will be doing life
without parole. Waiting to go up north,
with nothing to lose but time. This thug
looking mother fucker who is a convicted
rapist. He is always talking about getting
an appeal on a federal level. Studying on
how to get his conviction over turned.
He will be expedited soon. He
knew the feds was coming to
get his ass. I knew he had more
than a rape charge. He just
would not say, what the Feds
wanted him for. I would just
listen to him. He's a big dude.
I knew he could bench press
me for wreck. It's disgusting to
see man who loves to be fucked
by men. I wake up with a hard
on and hold my dick all the way
to the shower. It's crazy, living
with gay mother fuckers! Who
are only gay when the come to
jail. I have nothing against gay
people. It's not fun when you're
incarcerated and have to hold
on to your manhood. I'm tired
of being striped search. Lined
up in a line, with other naked
inmates. My dick and balls

La'Rahz - Roslyn O'Flaherty Isaacs

hanging in the front. While the
officer tells me to bend over spread
my cheeks and cough. I think these
mother fuckers get off on this shit.
As soon as I'm asked to strip and
bend I just lose it! I just ask the
same question. I don't know why
you want to see my dick all the time?
What you want me to, rub my nuts
for you. I am always being removed
off the line. The officers stay write me
up. I'm just not with that bending shit.
Jail makes it easy to become rebellious.
Right about now I don't give a fuck! I
feel it is so degrading for a man to look,
up another man ass. I wonder who else
is being, housed in my dorm. I will man
up and protect myself if necessary. I
made a weapon to defend myself. I'll jig
a mother fucker! I thought I made an
ingenious weapon. I'm starting to think,
was a weapon a good idea? I know that
if I stab someone. I can catch a new
charge. I'm trying to identify with my new
struggle. Realizing I now had a reason
to be disturbed and live in fear. I'm not
no bitch, but violence took place on the
dorms all the time. This doesn't justify
taking someone's life. I have to let a
mother fucker know. I am not the one,
they want to be fucking with. In my
eyes I was innocent. I was not a criminal,
like all theses other inmates.
Now I realize this isn't the time to be
incarcerated. A old man told me, to meet
him in the law library. He would show
me how to study up, on my case. So I
can get a better lawyer. He said I

needed an 18B lawyer. I really can't
believe my moms won't help me. She
won't put anything in my commissary.
I can forget about her send me any
clothes or sneakers. I had to get
clothes and slippers from the facility
clothes box. Inmates would leave me
clothing, when it was time for them to
be released. My moms had to be sick
of me and the bull shit that goes with it.
I know she acknowledges me as the son
she raised. I need some slot time on the
phone. I have to get in touch with this girl.
We are fuck buddies! I like her because
she has a fat ass. I guess if I step up my
game and tell her, I love her. Then all I have
to do is convince her, that she is Wifey. Then
she will visit me and bring me care packages
on a regular basis. Wifey will keep my
commissary full. Wifey is living large on the
streets. She is going to do this bid with me. I
found a job in jail making twenty five cents a
hour, sweeping and mopping. I only get three
hours a day. Do the math! Is this slave wages
or what? The institution calls it a honest living.
The job keeps me off the dorms and out of
trouble. I need the money for stamps and
envelopes to write my lawyer. It's a damn
shame that it took all this to happen to me
for me to believe.
THIS ISN'T THE TIME TO JAIL!

MINIMUM WAGE BUM

You're my minimum wage
bum. You can't make it to
work everyday and get a
full paycheck. You wonder
why we don't have anything?
I'm spending your money. It
has your personality, cheap.
You won't even pay your child
support. Only a jack ass would
forget to support their son!
The judge wants you to start
sending money to your son.
You're a dead beat dad. Take
care of your responsibility. No
one should have to tell you to
support your child.
One sure way to satisfy the
situation is for you to get a
second job. Non payment of
child support can lead to
incarnation. Worked Ten
years on a part time job with no
overtime. You use to scramble
on the streets. Now you're
talking about going to the
food stamp office. A bum
on food stamps, because his
wages are to low.
ARE YOU KIDDING ME?
Food stamps are not the
solution. Minimum wages
is not getting it Boo. Own
up to your responsibility.
You can excel above your
expectations. I keep telling

you to further your education.
So you can have a better
future. Did you ever think,
about working full time every
day? I think you're just set
in your ways. I am underwhelmed
by you. I try to motivate you. What
happened to self determination. I'm
starting to believe, you like making
minimum wage. Holler at me when
you get yourself together!

BRUTAL DEATH

Brutal death, they killed my
baby ran up in my shit. Just shot
him dead. Gave him a severe harsh
beaten. Gang bangers living in their
world of organized crime. Savages
real cruel individuals. Just heartless
without regard to God or Jesus.
My son killed disrespected, assaulted
and murdered by uncivilized thugs.
Various ethnic gangs with territorial
boundaries. They just kicked
in my front door. Violated my home,
my son died a brutal assignation.
He had home boys with so call gang
intelligence. Where were they, when
it came time to help my son? Could
they have set him up? They loved
the fantasy of armed conflict. Street
gangs with lack of consideration for
others is what killed my child. He
was shot, stabbed and beaten beyond
recognition. My son lays six feet under
covered with earth. I'm still paying my
friend back for burying him. Monetary
gifts were greatly appreciated. My baby
boy's life not even acknowledged by,
gang members or big time drug dealers.
They did not give their condolences or
support to me. I guess he should not
have trusted his peers. He needed to
be a leader with good intentions, not a
follower. My foundation of Strength
and my support came from my friends.
My child's death stayed on my mind. A
senseless killing. To murder my

son wasn't a revelation from God.
My son wasn't doing the right
thing. He lived in a single parent
household. Was all the nurturing skills
needed from me enough? He decided
gangs and violence made him a man.
This fight, he really didn't want it. He
couldn't even bring it. I don't wish
senseless death on no one. I looked
for government officials help. To
sanction punishment for disobedience.
My son above the law, now lying
beyond the grave. Maybe he should
have gone to jail. Convicted for being
associated with criminals, with felony
offences. I wonder if jail would have
kept him alive. I could have accepted
that punishment, better than him
being dead. My mind was
destroyed by the death of my
son. His unquestionable lifestyle
and principles were made with his
conscious decision. I wonder if he
was fearful of his assassination?
Sometime I felt he didn't have any
fear in his heart. My son stressed
me out with his gang family. We
went for family counseling and he
was able to con the therapist. She
stated this year we will work on him.
He will be able to manage life
situations. Her book smarts was not
helping my child. He still was unable
to think his way, out of the box and
execute a plan to better his life.
She truly didn't have any street
smarts. She was to damn cocky to
see past her title. I believed every

thing the therapist told me. I sign
papers to agree to her long term
goal. I stayed in court trying to get
court official to mandate my son to
a group home. Until he could be
properly evaluated. I needed him
off the streets. Nothing was being
done about it. I work every day and
pay taxes. I feel the system failing my
son and let me down. A brutal death
a real ruthless situation occurred. My
only child is dead. He took his existence
of being a gang member to his grave.
The incident remains under investigation.
As a mother I don't condone violence.
Adult leadership in our communities
can help our young ethnic minorities.
It time to take our streets back and
transform our community. Stop letting
violence goes on in our own back yard.
My sons' street level loyalty and sacrifices
as being a low life gangster. Stressed me
out physically and mentally. Who will stand
up and advocate for our youth? The future lies
in young people and their future is in trouble.

SUBSTANTIATE YOUR SITUATION

I am not the benefactor to
your pregnancy. My sperm
was not a charitable donation.
To you having a baby, I don't
care what you say. I'm not the
recipient for your child. Stop
telling people I'm your baby's
daddy. Your child will not be
welcomed or accepted as mine.
You see I have a family, my wife
and kids. I told you that on many
occasions. Child support will
bankrupt me, right about now.
I'm not monetary worth for you
and your fetus. So stop crying,
you can't exploit me. I can't
substantiate your situation.
Your mind set has to change.
Your situation has you living
in poverty and fear. This mind
blowing experience come from
a fundamental truth, lack of self
assurance. You have no personal
achievement, to change the way
your thinking. You were just a piece
of ass I can't afford. I barely can
support myself. I was just fucking you,
just to fuck! I wasn't looking for a baby
out of the deal. Your acting ignorant,
like a jackass. Leave me alone. This
situation is scandalous to me, fuck you . . .
YOU HANDLE IT!!!

XO XO

X's AND O's hugs and kisses
Your love has crossed my heart
with X's and O's.
        Smooth kisses,
        a gentle touch.
Your strength always welcomed.
The well being, I feel in this relationship
makes me worthy of X's and O's.
Platonic at this point.
Yes! Love, trust, happiness and contentment.
Your loves touches my heart with understanding.
I'll marry you, I'm happy you asked.
Your heart will never leave my soul,
cause the X's and O's came with
your trust. Till death do we part?
        I'm ready to start!
You see I was tired
of sex with benefits.
I was looking for
X's And O's.
Ultimate pleasure my
love has a choice.
Love and intimacy
is the road to cross.
I'm ready to cross
        X O X O
I am very unbending
about, the kind of
man I want to love.

NEW YEAR'S

Black eye peas,
white rice,
corn bread,
collard greens,
hog maws,
chitterlings
and
hot sauce!
Yes it's,
NEW YEARS EVE!
365 days have passed.
1 year older,
1year wiser,
Income tax time!
HAPPY NEW YEAR,
God Blessed You!
The ball has dropped.
Forty Second Street,
Time Square. The prices to
get in the club has doubled.
Your ready to bring the New
Years in with a bang. You
can't afford to hang. Your
mind wonder off and you start
thinking of your New Year's
Resolution. Your resolution for
this year is to work on some
of the ignorance in our society.
To keep the resolution
sometimes it's mind over
matter or it can have you
feeling something is the
matter with your mind!
You identify with the fact
that some ignorance in
society is learnt and your
resolution won't wear your
spirit down!

FATHER

I lost my father to his women,
drinking and drugging. I have
a strong desire for his acceptance.
How do I free myself from
the pain this brings. He's
not reaching out to me.
Is it a fantasy of the imagination
for me to have the ideal father?
Will there be peace with the past?
Should I hate my birth father? A
weak man making wrong decisions.
Why won't he contact me?
Some communication is
needed. I'm broken hearted!
I need to no he loves me. My
father's abandonment has
verbally, mentally and physically
battered me. Half ass monetary
court relationship was a
representation of love for awhile.
I need someone to acknowledge
my pain and hurt. Grandma's visits
are dead. I don't understand these
inappropriate family relationships
in my life. My father's alive why
can't we reconcile our relationship.
I forgive him. I love my father. I'm
trying to minimize the pain my
father cause's in my life. He really
doesn't want to be my father. So ill
claim him as my dad! "PHILIPPIANS: Charter-4
Verse-13 says, I can do all things through Christ
which strengthened me."

MOLESTED!!!

Molested as a child, intensive
sex. He overstepped his
boundary. EXPLOITED ME!
Took advantage of me selfishly.
I was a child. Utilized as his sex
toy. My family and friends consider
this an alleged affair.
I was looking for salvation. This is
their psychological profile. I don't
want to be the cause of family
confusion. I need to be able to
escape my daily life. With a
unstrained imagination. Coming
to terms with my pass. I think of
myself as a new embryo in life,
because of the perception of
past issues. Transformation from
pain for me and my family has
been hard. A real power struggle,
over placing guilt and blame.
Devastated, I try not to let my
life crash down before me.
I will be brave and change my
moody temper and disposition.
These toxic emotions of
depression has scared my
spirit and soul. I pray for
strength and guidance.
I want other's to learn
from my experience.
Beware of the Rape-per-man he is out there.
He preys on men, women and children!

MY FUCK FACE

My baby loves
to talk
during
intercourse.
Yes, while we
make passionate
love.
Once he asked me,
come on baby let
me see what your fuck
face looks like.
the deeper he put it in,
I lost control
over my facial expression.
Was this the face,
I was to unveil
to him? A rear
expression while we
lay together. I watched
an erection that oozed of
confidence. Not even
started all the way he
could already tell what
my fuck face looked like.
Emotionally and physically
he slammed deeper into
my soul than I could imagine.
It just wasn't
all about a
fuck face to me!
I'll show him my
ecstasy face.
My face what it
looked like, when
he pulled out and
he started whacking
his Dick!

THE DRAFT

Government draftee, soldiers
selected for assignment.
For military services.
Ma Ma's baby boy
Now Uncle Sam's war ploy.
War on the battle front.
The arm forces in [HIGH GRASS 4 FEET TALL,
            THE ENEMY JUMPING OUT OF
                THICK UNDER BUSH,
                POST TRAUMATIC STRESS,
                    DIRT ROADS,
                    FOX HOLES,
                    PRISON CAMPS,
            CORPSE AND ENEMY SNIPERS,
                    BOMBS,
            TROOPS BEING AMBUSHED]
[ENEMY BULLETS HITTING THE GROUND,
            TEARS, RAIN, BLOOD
            AND DAMAGED SOULS
                MILITARY MEN!!!]
Stratagem for government
killing innocent victims
and the enemy.
Your friends
and family in the
military movement.
Time to properly give back to the
survivors of our nation. Who have
come home having, nightmares
where they wake up fighting in
their sleep. Believing that their
still in enemy territory. When
will the wars stop in their head.
Imagine having a baby and
having to leave it on enemy soil.

La'Rahz - Roslyn O'Flaherty Isaacs

As you continue to live your
patriotic duty. Spiritual healing
is needed as soldiers return home
and live the next chapter of their
life. Receiving recognition from
our nation, their families and
friends. Love given to mommy
and daddies baby boy.
Families reunited in military cemeteries'
taps blown,
gun shots fired,
flag honored the deceased!
Veteran Administration Hospital
treats some military men like 2nd
class citizens.
shell shocked,
alcoholics,
limbs lost,
internal problems,
strung out junkies,
psychiatric patients
with
psychotic personalities!
Homes and choices of jobs
are limited for our military men.
They should not live in shame!!!
For they are our WAR HEROES!!!
Honored on Veterans day. The
draft will soon return so the
government can enlist military
men. Some military men will be
dedicated to fight a war they really
don't understand. They will go into
combat with dignity. Why is war our
billion dollar industry. I wonder if the
president, can put a stop to the draft.
Will Supreme Court have the higher
power? "GOD BLESSES AMERICA"

DEAR MR. PRESIDENT

I am your ex-draftee. I returned home
from enemy soil. I feel like I have
taken a bullet from our economic
system. I'm suffering from a system
that is not for the poor. I am just another
statistic, silenced and feeling like I don't
belong. To draw a conclusion on ethics
is a bit overwhelming. Has American
power destroyed this great nation and
the American dream. Does the decisions
made for our country come from you or
supreme court. Have we went from
justice to injustice. What should I believe?
I was not sure where to address this letter.
I have arrived home from the war with the
purple heart. Life has buried my heart.
I believe my injuries earned me the
purple heart. I served with my the
infantry. I wound up in a blood bath
with the foot soldiers that died
on this search and destroy
mission. Your American hero is
indigent! World ethics has me
bound to capitalism. I am living
like I'm in the great depression.
One war was enough. I question
who motivated the bank to take
my home in foreclosure. I returned
from the war homeless. I have
nothing to call my own, except the
memories of killing individuals. The
smell of death blood and burnt bodies.
Troop's blood slippery under my feet.
A fight in which I hold within myself.
I can't get rid of these images. Shell

La'Rahz - Roslyn O'Flaherty Isaacs

shocked in my dreams of the dead
and the wounded. Terror lies in my
heart as my mind scatters for needed
growth. To overcome intense fear of
the enemies ammunition and booby
traps. I must believe that when I
took a life. It was the enemy that had
to be killed or they would murder your
troops. I served my country. My mind
is destroyed over the fact that I am
homeless. Was Wall Street waiting for
me. The path they put me on just lead
to failure. The stock market—BOWS
DOWN TO THE BLOOD OF JESUS!
I live in the Bowery. In New York City
under a bridge. Mr. President
feel free to look for me. When
you get a chance. I thought my
purple heart would show me the
right to equality and justice. I
was unguided by authorized
representatives. I was thinking that
our government communication
would exercise my right. I didn't
understand the politics. I am living
a heritage of self destruction!!!
Well the empathy is gone. I have
to get my self together. The best
way I can. I was looking for a great
humanitarian for relief. Hoping they
would act in the interest of the
people with righteousness. Well I
better have faith and trust in myself.
I won't let myself down. God has
empowered myself determination.
I have new found confidence.
That I found in praise. The Lord
gave me discernment. It is

making my heart strong with
endless possibilities for change.
I found something to call my
own. I pray in church with my
church family. Yet I feel like a
victim of injustice. As I put my
money in the collection plate.
I watch funds being misused
by people who say they have
the calling from God. I love my
church family. I don't speak of
the misappropriated funds. I
don't sow to the people. I sow
to God. I question why my church
has a ATM machine at the front
entrance. Well I'm living new
beginnings. Although honorable
discharge from the war still
only makes me feel like I'm
living on the front line, on
government soil. I was drafted
into this wars confrontation. My
purple heart has become a symbol
with no substance. Sometimes I
wonder if many troops became
disillusioned with a vivid memory
of what the draft was all about.
Did they think the war would not
effect them because they returned
home. Were they still bound to the
wars destruction. I took my tears,
fears and prayers to the Lord.
While trying to understand the
6th Commandment.
KJV 1987 by Thomas Nelson
(Exodus—Chapter 20 verse 13
says:) "THOU SHALL NOT KILL"
Mr. president was this really our

La'Rahz - Roslyn O'Flaherty Isaacs

war? Well Mr. President thank
you for allowing me to use my
first amendment rights and the
freedom to understand life's
precedents, however manifested.
I am looking for the New York
Department Of Justice to monitor
my civil rights. This will help
me give respect where respect is
due. As I rectify my outstanding
problems. That I need to address
to military personnel. I end my letter
but not my love for our troops and
this great nation. In this war of
oppression they called me a
draftee, but I am a vessel of God.

VANILLA OR CHOCOLATE

Vanilla State
And
Chocolate City
not able to endure poverty.
It has become intolerable.
The deficiency of being poor.
Feeling like a slave in New York.
Domination of an inadequate
precipitation created by
authorities and institutions.
Theatrical politics
and so call equal rights.
Lifting me up, enabling me to
hold positive strength with
a level of inconstancy.
Mutual respect for
my life's intellectual
movement. While I
live urban horror.
I guess its subject
to change or a
alternative is needed.
I can't expose myself to
the criticism about this
VANILLA
OR
CHOCOLATE
CITY . . .

ONE ICE COLD MOLEY AND PHONE BONE CUMMING UP

Phone Bone,
yeah,
I'm going to have me some.
Get this mutha fucka on
the bone.
While I masturbate.
A jet stream of cum
between my legs.
A sensational feeling,
delivered while he
phone bones me.
"Boy" I get hot
just thinking about
2 individuals
conversing.
The assumed feeling
of releasing on my
panties. As I played
with myself. Getting
my shit off, while I
screamed Awww!
Bonding over the phone
in sexual conversation.
Afterwards I have one
ice cold moley. I'm going
to relax the rest of the
day. Until he can give
me one hard tasty
boner. I have to keep
it Cuming.

DADDY

Daddy,
never hugged me.
A nightmare with
a stress level.
Human contact
and no affection. Allowed
me to call him Dad, when
he wanted to be a dictator.
After I turned 14 years old.
I never saw him again. I could
not continue to look for him.
I compromised my morals trying
to do what my mom thought
was proper. For our father and
son relationship. My mom isn't
a man she'll never no how I feel.
I don't even have my father's
last name. I wonder if he wanted
me in the first place. He was my
daddy, but I was forced to be the
male of the house. I didn't want a
father figure. My dad won't man
up and give me the parental
guidance that I need. I find it
difficult to communicate with my
father. I decided to continue my
life without my dad. I could no
longer look up to him. My dad
fucked my head up. I have to
protect my mind. It was crushed
by my dope feign father, needles—
foil—burnt spoons hidden in the
house. He's always looking for new
places to stash his works. So my
mother would not find them. My

La'Rahz - Roslyn O'Flaherty Isaacs

father start off snorting dope.
Next thing I knew he was a heroin
addict and I still loved him. My
moms kicked him out. He abused
her. Sold her body for dope. Beat
her black and blue. On a regular
basis. A fearful experience, drugs
dominated his life. His excuse for
his lifestyle was, he was always
misunderstood. By his parents he
was what is call the black sheep
of the family. My father told me he
was strung out. He did not love the
drug. He did it so he would not get
sick. Always scratching and nodding.
He had the mentality of a dope fiend.
I have my own opinion of him. He was
to damn selfish, with no morals. A very
perverse person. I was condemned by the
experience of the existing circumstances.
It's hard being the son of a, strung out junkie.
I could no longer watch the man I loved,
beg and lie for money. My dad turned
into a thief. Went to jail on several
occasions. When he was released from
jail. My dad was still a junkie. He was
still using drugs in jail. He never stopped
his friends would bring him dope on the
days he was able to have jail visits. I
believe my father could shoot up in the
veins, in his neck and nuts, if he had to.
My dad has track marks on his
arms and feet. All the veins in his
legs have collapsed. His hands
are so swollen. I wonder if it hurts
when he closes his hand. Sleeping
on benches, roof tops and hallways.
Now that he lost his wages of

employment. The repo man has
taken his car. The only thing in
his life he really loves.
Dope administered, suffering to our
family. Methadone program just kept
him relapsing and going in the hospital.
When he was clean he was a ladies
man living from house to house. Never
getting his own crib. His women
would keep him with a car. Well
dressed until he gets that monkey,
on his back again. His life
is one big withdrawal. With a
obscure personality disorder,
constantly showing destructive
behavior. He has a narcissist
complex. I don't have to condone his behavior.
Yes, my Moms raised me; I am a testimony of life.
Now that I am a forgiving person I understand my
parents love me. I am content within myself.
"Psalm 51 verses 7 and 8 says,
7 purge me with hyssop, and I shall be clean:
wash me, and I shall be whiter than snow.
8 Make me to hear joy and gladness: that the
Bones which thou hast broken may rejoice"

MANURE CAUSES FINANCIAL SUICIDE

*Mr. Government officials. Are
we really broke or is all this
propaganda. Warranted to
allow the people. To attach
themselves to the manure
that causes financial suicide.
The management of limited
funds, is the financial suicide
with manure strangling me.
Bill collectors messing with
me. The phone company
demanding payment. There's
no money to be made. Pushed
around on extensions from
unemployment. Why do the
bill collectors have such a nasty
attitudes. With uncooperative
dispositions. I explain the
economy is really bad.
I have no one to supply me with
money or capital gain. Twenty year
old saving bonds worthless. IRA
accounts are manure now. Manure
causing the silent voices. Effected
by the well running dry. Language
needed to pave the way for others.
I'm living part of me is dead, my
monetary resources. Liberal policy
on education makes damaging
choices.
The Constitution is gone from
my life. Lobbyist writing laws,
inducted into nonsense social
structure. Time to reach a
common ground in our culture.
I can't let all this stuff consume
me. Student loan, I claimed hard-*

ship deferment. I have no
hospital coverage for my family.
I hope the health care reform
doesn't have any flaws. In my
opinion it should be in the best
interest of all people. Who and
what will it actually affect? Child
support not enough. Before
unemployment, I lived paycheck
to paycheck. Yes' I'm living and
drowning in manure. I need to be
debt free. With a new credit rating
the management of no money is
intentionally killing me.
Between my credit cards ratings
bank account and mortgage. I
have too many battle scars. I
face my financial problems
with dignity and pride. People
have told me that this is a
recession. It's not mine I
have been birthed into this
situation. I will not speak
recession into my life. I know
how to eat beans with out swine.
Victimized in the political attitudes
and explicit languages of society.
I'm compromised with frustration.
That's trying to pull the foundation
from under me. I always manage to
live above the manure. I'm not
acting like my shit doesn't stink. I no
my bowels, smell like manure.
God gave me two arms two
feet and a brain. To think out
the box. The unspoken word
is the silent majority. Freedom
of speech and minorities want
to kill that noise about recession
manure as we watch the economy shift.
        I'M INDIGENT LIVING ECONOMIC DEFERMENT!!!

LET'S GET IT POPPN'

You're always trying to rent
space in my head. I have
no power over my life. You
managed to work the trail
and tribulation of the two evils.
Exposing me to your shit and
making me a alternative to the
bull shit. I was exploring the
possibility of change and no
more mischief
       YIELD!
I have the right away,
right about now. Lets
eliminate the nonsense.
Let's get it on and poppn.

I LIVE IN VIETNAM

Vietnam gang related turmoil
existing without regard or
thoughts of others. They threw
pit bulls off the roof for recreation.
Gun shots out hallway window.
When you walk out the building.
You just hit the ground because
bullets are flying. Dead bodies
found in stair wells. Gang
morality taking law into its own
hand. Upsetting function and
structure of neighborhoods. Is
redemption possible! Poverty
broken homes with juveniles
on probation engaging in turf wars.
Is justification needed to stop gang
members. It is time to suppress
their activities. Their not going
anywhere. Will they ever take
responsibility for their actions.
Should they be ostracized from
society? Tattoos should be
removed by parents. Tattoos
being used to identify juveniles
and gang members. Walking
tattoo bill boards. Identification
for cops or society to label
them. Gang parents and children
living in the lack of the law
and order. Our babies on the
computer throwing up gang
signs and they can't even pea
straight. Minors half naked,
smoking refer and don't realize job
and legal official use there web page

to determine their character and the
temperament of their personality.
Public disturbances and confusion.
Poverty a ruthless priority, with no pity
or compassion. Is this a form of love?
Our love ones mentally, physically and
spiritually damaged. Once in a gang
you can't get out. Life as a soldier trap
in the threat of death. Is this the short
lived, life that we want for our youth.
Juvenile girls having gang babies. Our
infants incarcerated at birth. Being raised
in jail with their mother. Freedom in
the air. Not on my street, Vietnams
is still here. Foot soldier in the hood
incarcerated at 18 years of age doing
adult time. Are our children listening
to their inner self when the decide to
join a gang. Is love the internal feeling
coming from their gang leaders. As
they live in a code of silence. When is
realism going to set in that Vietnam on
the streets are not their war.

CRACK CITY

Crack city,
the walking
dead. The city
never sleeps.
The chetta
disappear as
rocks burn.
You got it
twisted thinking
this all in my
mind.
I sold my
twat.
For the craving
of crack.
I always wanted
the big rock,
not crumbs.
I lay on my back
an became what
I despised most.
Yes I was a crack
whore. I have to
deter from all the
men I'm sleeping
around with. If
they allow me to
fuck them I will.
I have to hit the
pipe. That glass

dick. I didn't care
that I was living
like I lacked
intelligences. Just
relieving the
addiction. My ass
was the abrupt end
of this mission.
I became homeless
While I lived in Crack
City . . .

GROWN ADULT

Eager to be an adult. Thinking
you've arrived at full maturity.
Fully developed but not fully
aged. Sneaking around in
bars so men can Mack to
you. Sitting on the stool
almost passed out. Acting
like a fool. Feeling like your
grown. Not living on your
own. You wind up at some
jerks house. Just to shack
up. Not thinking about teen
pregnancy. Before you can
get your skirt off. 10 inches
was swinging in your face.
Yes! That's what adults bring.
Your naive and can't even
holler back. Cause now he's
ready to put something
between your lips. You ask,
why people call you trashy?
You went on line. There you
was buck naked in an erotic
web cam show. You have
low self esteem. This
behavior cannot give you
inspired confidence. You
really should not be sexually
open as a grown adult. Reach
beyond your comfort zone. It's
possible to achieve what you
truly deserve. A peace of mind,
with happiness and love. You
should be eternally grateful
to live pass your dark past.
Keep your mouth shut and your
legs closed! You are not a adult.
You are just a young lady . . .

La'Rahz - Roslyn O'Flaherty Isaacs

BEAT DOWN

I can't take another beat down
to this external punishment. My
husband out of control. He got that
killer Swag. He loves me?
This controlling man is ridiculing
me. With wrong improper abusive
behavior, always hospitalizing me.
Cops don't even entertain situation
in their mind. Disregarded court
order lying in my dwelling. I still
take ass whippings. Opposed to
my husband receiving jail time.
I can only live one day at a time.
I hope I stop living in this
condemnation to hell. I
dread the day I have to
whip out the court order of
protection. Due to the next
beat down. I have to stop
hiding the improper abuse.
I feel like my heart is minutes
away from deaths door.

GOD GIVES YOU THE FREEDOM WITH ALTERNATIVES . . .

"JAMES CHAPTER 2 Verse 17says,
'Even so faith, if it the hath not works is dead, being alone." JAMES Chapter-4
Verse-7 says, submit yourselves, therefore to God. Resist the devil, and he will
flee from you."

> **Dear Lord,**
> **I belong to you mind, body and soul.**
> **Please don't allow the Devil to take**
> **over me. Amen!**
>
> **La'Rahz R.E.O.I.**

YOU ARE BEING BLESSED

*You can't continue to live in
fear. You have choices in
life. Faith in the Holy Spirit
will save your morals and
principals. You are being
blessed in the seed of love.
pray that loyalty and love
can change the world. We
need to have passionate
affections for people feelings.
Help give them the ability to
bear hardship and pain.
Walk with Jesus with faith,
confidence and love.
Believe if you do this you will
get total praise from God and
be delivered from your problems.
Spiritual confidence and guidance
will be the glory of God. Deliverance
from the worlds damnation and
eternal punishment. Is the mercy
you will endure forever. To continue
suffering is not Gods will. Thank
God for answering your prayers.
Give your life to Jesus Christ.
He will give you peace and praise.
God does not condemn you. Jesus
died for your sins. Sometimes self
leadership makes people want to
be God. The father, the son and
the Holy Spirit is love. You have
to plant the seed to make it grow.
Perseverance is the story of life.
That brings out character and
change through the Holy Spirit.*

Try not to live in condemnation.
Hopelessness does not give you
faith. Independent living send
some people in a spiritual direction.
God will deal with you for your
wrong doings. He is a forgiving
God. We have the choice to repent
for our sins. To live in distant from
God with a condescending spirit is
not love. Man can't tell you about
death and damnation. They should
not speak this into your life. Don't
let man make you feel like your
not part of the body of Christ.
Go to the "WORD" to no who
God is. Fearing God is in the
Bible. The Fear of God is not
a sin. The enemy makes you
fear things. The blood of Jesus
prevails. Believe you are
blessed in the name of
Jesus. Don't be mislead
In your season.

A LITTLE PIECE OF HEAVEN

*Mama always gave me a
little piece of heaven. Her
honesty and integrity was
held in high respect.
Shared her time
heart, money
and smiles!
Never judging me all the
while. I contracted her
emotions. She kept my
butt out of trouble. Even
when I was wrong.
Her love always made
my character strong.
Honor and wisdom is a
great quality of her love.
Grand children were from heaven
above. While I looked for integrity.
From my daughters dad. Mama
and me had a codependent
relationship. I lived my mother's
expectations and ideas. Thinking
her thoughts. While she lived her
life through mine. Subjected to
her rules while raising my family
in her household. Ma Ma's
psychological dependency on
me is abnormal. She needs to
go on with her life.
I need to be an adult and take
responsibility for me and my kids.
God's heavenly glory
is the respect of our individuality.
The season will touch our lives.
In a little piece of heaven.*

THE MIRACLE

The love in our heart,
    Through
faith and mercy controls our
        lives.
Try to understand the
method of the Lord. The miracle
not to judge others. Will give
you energy in your soul to
live in grace. The Lord will
never condemn you. He
wants you to excel in life.
To make your life emotionally
content. You must believe
and receive him. It's time
to speak and teach the word
of obedience. Come now an
live the opportunity of a miracle.
You will not be convicted
through judgment. You
will live the seed of comfort.
For you are the miracles of
the Lord. He will always be
your father in heaven. The
gate to heaven is always
open, you were chosen to
be a vessel. You can find
peace with God and the
book of life . . .

THE BIBLE

I believe in God. Organized religion
is what I'm trying to understand.
Should religion be mixed with our government
affairs? Religion to me is a belief, and we all
have our own belief. Read the bible
for yourself. Let God interpret the
bible in your heart. God will manifest
the truth in your heart.
Your assignment is to spread Gods love.
Bring God souls. God will
show you the Holy Spirit.
In Jesus precious name Amen.
Your
walk
with
GOD
is
Personal . . .
No matter what street
you travel on this earth.
You are still a child
of the Lord.
You have a purpose
in life. Develop your
courage and believe it . . .

CONVERT TO THE LORD
AND HIS KINGDOM

Let us all give hope to those who live in disastrous conditions. Poverty stricken as they're struggling with what some call a recession. The dollars asset value is eroding. The representation of the dollar that is in circulation may change and have a new distribution of currency that some call the ditch dollar. This will be used in order to ruin the world. Economics is crippling us. The recession has focused on Foreclosures and lost wages that have made people homeless. There are bigger problems in the world. Why is our center of attention on diamond, gold and the newest fashions? Should this be the encouragement of love in our heart. That is being used to nurture our young. This will not be found in the Lord kingdom. It is used to keep us blind on what is really happening in the world and the problems that we really need deliverance from. Why is college education making our graduating students over qualified for employment. They are forced to flip burgers for a living. Why are colleges and jails our billion dollar industries. Take a look at our health plans. We can't afford to go to the doctor. Why are we being forced to pay co-payment? Just to see the doctors and co-payment to get results from previous doctor visit. A co-payment that continue to remind you that. You can live or die by the sword in health care. Senior citizen have worked all their lives now have to pay for Medicare part B. Many soldiers have served in the armed forces. They are now on Social Security hungry with nutritional deficiencies. Water bills are being paid by home owners. Should they have to buy bottle water? In order to have fresh water to drink. Human kind is in a water war. Who would ever think the world could be taken over with water. That the Lord provided us with. The filth and pollution is not a unplanned mistake. Man will be drilling for water some day as we live in the land of the rich and thirsty. The economy is in a financial turmoil. What is the tax code for the super rich. Hiding their money overseas. The rich should be willing to pay taxes and stop feeling the only thing they should do is investing money to benefit themselves. Weather conditions are bad (global warming?) as we suffer with climate disruption. People struggle to live through hurricane and tornadoes storms. Heat waves killing people. Fires are destroying our land. Is the ozone layer a danger to us? The earth is also being controlled with urban floods. Conditions that are impacting people's cultures, leaving them in doubt of unsure futures. Lower levels of water turning into droughts. People suffering they are thirsty. Corporations selling water to the poor. Times are coming were only the rich will, always have fresh water. Mosquitoes giving humans viruses that kill. People suffering with bed bugs in their schools and dwellings. Epidemic of rats are taking over our neighborhood and train stations. Animals are becoming extinct throughout the world. Our nation fights wars that we don't understand. I question why we fight the same way in our neighborhoods. We struggle to live in our lost society as we look for world peace. Our civilization is declining. The Lord is waiting, for us to see past our troubles. We are all miracle. Have we all sinned in one way or another? God loves us even when were dirty and stinking. A Kingdom Of Controversy is a kingdom of thought. Not written to belittle anyone. It was written to let us look at different situations. That we turn our heads to and stick our nose up at, as we call ourselves people of God. I hope we can live in a "no judgment zone." This will enable Gods children to come to church and fellowship with others. It takes a village to raise a child. Should we give our perception on what love, truth and realty are? Yet we speak what we feel should be the norm for the lost souls. That some have cast away from the church, because they are fighting with their own demons. Is it of God for a church family to glorify themselves, as they look for self gratification in Jesus name Amen? I guess some people feel they get the glory for that. Is it right to use idolatry while worshiping with religion. Don't let our convictions be a dance with the devil and his dictatorship. The gift of life is truly forgiveness. Jesus says in John chapter 5 verse 39 and 40. 39-Search the scriptures; for in them ye think ye have eternal life and they are they which testify of me. 40-And ye might not come to me, that he might have life. Do you really have the calling from God? **A Kingdom of Controversy** was also written for those who don't acknowledge that hard times in our lives exist. La'Rahz writes not to bring you out of Gods salvation. She wants you to know that, God gives you freedom with options. She hopes this book can save souls. The victory is truly upon us. We must no, we will make it and that God gets the glory for us being delivered, from the penalty of our sins. We must be patient. God knows your heart!

DON'T HATE ME 'CAUSE YOU AIN'T ME

I LOVE EVERYONE, HATER ALERT . . . I am not my past
So don't claim it for yourself. It is what it is, the past . . .
Be enlightened
by the knowledge in the Bible . . .

"MATTHEW: CHAPTER 24, VERSE 12 says,
"And because iniquity shall abound,
the love of many shall wax cold."

VERSE 13 says,
"But he that shall endure unto the end,
the same shall be saved."
When I go to heaven, God's not going to ask me
what church I came from. The Lord will ask
What did I do in his name?
Did I do what he called me to do?
Was he in my heart and did I love Him? He
is not even going to ask who my church leader is!

La'Rahz ~ R.E.O.I.
Story telling poet . . .

LA'RAHZ ENDS HER KINGDOM OF CONTROVERSY

To focus on becoming a cancer survivor.
Where is our spiritual walk to faith?
Time to be delivered from the Kingdom of
Controversy. This is not God's Kingdom.
My father in heaven said we will be alright.
Time to get into the Word. The Word
is faith from God.
I thank God for waiting for me;
I must leave my troubles
in God's hands.
I believe he does not like a whole lot of mess.
God loves me and I must let something go.
God gets the glory,
His will be done.

"MARK: CHAPTER 11 VERSE 22 says,
"And Jesus answering saith unto them, have faith in God."
A Kingdom Of Controversy is not God's Kingdom.
A Kingdom Of Controversy is a kingdom of thought!
God gives you a destiny with free-will! Awe freedom to choice.
The bondage that hold our souls needs prayer!

GOD'S KINGDOM IS GODS GOVERNMENT THAT WILL RULE THE EARTH . . .

Acts 1 verse 8 says
> But ye shall receive power, after that the Holy Ghost is come upon you: and ye shall be witness unto me both in Je-ru-sal-em, and in all Ju-dae-a, and in Sa-ma'-ri-a and unto the utter most part of the earth.

Act 5 verse 42—says
> And daily in the temple, and in every house, they ceased not to teach and preach Je'-sus Christ.

Luke 21 verse 7 says
> And they asked him, saying, Master, but when shall these things be? And what sign will there be when these things shall come to pass?

Luke 21 verse 10 says
> Then said he unto them, Nation shall rise against nation, and kingdom against kingdom:

Luke 21 verse 28 says
> And when these things begin to come to pass, then look up, your heads; for your redemption drawe'th nigh.

Luke 21 verse 25 says
> And there shall be signs in the sun, and in the moon, and in the stars; and upon the earth distress of nation of nations with perplexity; the sea and the waves roaring;

Luke 21 verse 31 says
> So likewise Ye, when Ye see things come to pass, know Ye that the kingdom of God is nigh at hand.

La'Rahz - Roslyn O'Flaherty Isaacs

Daniel 2 verse 44 says

> And in the days of these Kings shall the Gods of heaven set up a kingdom, which shall never be destroyed: and the kingdom shall not be left to other people, but it shall break in pieces and consume all these kingdoms, and it shall stand for ever.

Luke 8 verse 1 says

> And it came to pass afterwards, that he went throughout every city and village, preaching and shewing the glad tidings of the kingdom of God: and the twelve were with him.

Mathews 6 verse 9 says

> After this manner therefore pray ye: Our Father which art in heaven. Hallowed be thy name.

Mathews 6 verse 10 says

> Thy kingdom come. Thy will be done in earth, as it is in heaven.

Mathews 24 verse 3 says

> And as he sat upon the mount of Olives, the disciples came unto him privately saying, Tell us, when shall these things be? And what shall be the sign of thy coming, and of the end of the world?

Mathew 24 verse 14 says

> And this gospel of the kingdom shall be preached in all the world for a witness unto all nations; and then shall the end come.

Mathews 24 verse 12 says

> And because iniquity shall abound, the love of many shall wax cold.

Mathews 24 verse 22 says

> And except those days should be shortened, there should no flesh be saved: but for the elect's sake those days shall be shortened.

Mathews 18 verse 18 says

> Verily I say unto you. Whatsoever ye shall bind on earth shall be bound in heaven and whatsoever ye shall loose on earth shall be loosed in heaven.

Mathews 18 verse19 says
> Again I say unto you. That if two of you shall agree on earth as touching any thing that they shall ask, it shall be done for them of my father which is in heaven.

Mathews 18 verse 20 says
> For where two or three are gathered together in my name, there am I in the midst of them.

1st John 5 verse 9 says
> And we know that we are of God, and the whole world lieth in wickedness.

Genesis 2 verse 17 says
> But of the tree of the knowledge of good and evil, thou shalt not eat of it: for in the day that thou eatest thereof thou shalt surely die.

Genesis 3 verse 1 says
> Now the serpent was more subtil than any beast of the field which the lord God had made, And he said unto the woman Yea, hath God said. Ye shall not eat from the tree of the garden?

Genesis 3 verse 2 says
> And the woman said unto the serpent. We may eat of the fruit of the trees of the garden:

Genesis 3 verse 3 says
> But of the fruit of the tree which is in the midst of the garden. God hath said, Ye shall not eat of it neither. Shall ye touch it lest ye die.

Genesis 3 verse 5 says
> For God doth know that in the day ye eat thereof, then your eyes shall be opened, and ye shall be as gods knowing good and evil.

Mathew 24 verse 21 says
> For then shall be great tribulation, such as was not. Since the beginning of the world to this time, no, nor ever shall be.

La'Rahz - Roslyn O'Flaherty Isaacs

Mathew 28 verse 18 says

> *And Jesus came and spake unto them, saying, all power is given unto me heaven and in earth.*

Mathew 28 verse 19 says

> *Go ye therefore, and teach all nations, baptizing them in the name of the Father and of the son, and of the Holy Ghost:*

Mathews 28 verse 20 says

> *Teach them to observe all things whatsoever I have commanded you: and, lo, I am with you always, even unto end the world A-men.*

1 Corinthians 8 verse 5 says

> *For though there be that are called gods. Whether in heaven or in earth. (as there be gods many, and lords many.*

Roman 5 verse 10 says

> *For if when we were enemies, we were reconciled to God by the death of his son, much more being reconciled, we shall be saved by his life.*

Roman 5 verse 11 says

> *And not only so, but we also joy in God through our Lord Jesus Christ, by who we have now received the atonement.*

Roman 5 verse 12 says

> *Wherefore, as by one man sin entered into the world, and death by sin; and so death passed upon all men, for that all have sinned:*

Roman 5 verse 13 says

> *(For until the law sin was in the world: but sin is not imputed when there is no law.*

John 17 verse 3 says

> *And this is life eternal, that they might know thee the only true God and Jesus Christ, whom thou hast sent.*

Revelation 1 verse 5

> *And from Je-sus Christ, who is the faithful witness, and the first begotten of the dead, and the prince of the kings of the earth. Unto him that loved us. And washed us from our sins in his blood.*

Act 5 verse 28 says

> *Saying, Did not we straitly command you that ye should not teach in this name? and, behold ye have filled Je-ru-sa-lem with your doctrine, and intend to bring this man's blood upon us.*

Act 5 verse 29 says

> *Then Pe'-ter and the others apostles answered and said, we ought to obey God rather than men.*

Mathews 7 verse 13 says

> *Enter ye in at the strait gate: for wide is the gate and broad is the way, that leadeth to destruction, and many there be which go in threat:*

Mathews 7 verse 14 says

> *Because strait is the gate, and narrow is the way which leadeth unto life, and few there be that find it.*

Mathews 7 verse 21 says

> *Not everyone that saith unto me. Lord Lord, shall enter into the kingdom of heaven; but he that doeth the will of my father which is in heaven.*

Mathew 7 verse 22 says

> *Many will say to me in that day Lord Lord, have we not prophesied in thy name? and in thy name have cast out devils? and in thy name done many wonderful work?*

GOD IS THE UNIVERSAL RULER.
THIS IS GOD'S GOVERNMENT.
A-MEN . . .

REFERENCES

Thomas Nelson
"The Holy Bible"
King James Version, REVISED 1987.

Thanks so much for your support.

A KINGDOM OF CONTROVERSY

*Being held hostage in that plantation
mentality is a great enslavement. This
is not our earthly mission . . .
The story telling poet La'Rahz writes
to liberate people. A Kingdom Of
Controversy has amorous poetry that
is for adults. La'Rahz says it's time to
stop living in exile and hopes
A Kingdom Of Controversy
can revive life. This book should be
internalized when read. R.E.O.I. gives
this book five stars!*

Printed in the United States
by Baker & Taylor Publisher Services